Glass Blowing

A TECHNICAL MANUAL

Glass Blowing

A TECHNICAL MANUAL

Ed Burke

THE CROWOOD PRESS

First published in 2005 by
The Crowood Press Ltd
Ramsbury, Marlborough
Wiltshire SN8 2HR

www.crowood.com

This impression 2010

British Library Cataloguing-in-Publication Data
A catalogue record for this book is available from the British Library.

ISBN 978 1 86126 521 0

Illustration previous page: 'Dunes' by Anthony Stern.

Typefaces used: text, Stone Sans; headings, Frutiger;
chapter headings, Rotis Sans.

Typeset and designed by
D & N Publishing
Lowesden Business Park, Hungerford, Berkshire.

Printed and bound in India by Replika Press Pvt. Ltd.

CONTENTS

Preface 7

E+M Glass: DOODLE TUMBLER.

PREFACE

No one who has witnessed hot, molten glass being blown to shape could fail to be fascinated and enthralled by the process. A chance meeting with molten glass at college in my home town of Sunderland was to change my life. While on my way to a lecture, I walked past an open door and was astonished by the noise and excitement within. I was transfixed, I stared in amazement through the doorway. The rumble of the huge gas burners, the white glow of the furnace, the perspiration on the brow of the makers, smoke and ash billowing up to the ceiling as they breathed life into the glass. From the most basic of raw materials – sand – an endless array of objects was being made, limited only by the imagination of the craftsmen at work. The juxtaposition of colour, clarity, transparency, opalescence, iridescence, reflectiveness and refractiveness was just stunning. The glassmakers were exploiting these sympathetic but contrasting qualities with their stunningly dexterous skills. I wanted to join in; I needed to join in. This was one of my life's defining moments. The glassmaking wizards were weaving their spells, pulling me towards them. As I walked through the door, my life began to change, every step of the process was shrouded in wonderment and I longed to have their secrets revealed to me.

The skilful manipulation of the qualities of glass has created some of the most wonderful objects known to man. Since its first discovery, thousands of years ago, glass has inspired craftsmen and artists to reach new heights. As the first man blew into glass down a hollow tube, at the time of the Roman empire, Pandora's box was being opened wider and wider. More and more techniques were being invented for the manipulation of this incredibly versatile material: blowing, bending, fusing, slumping, casting, *pâte de verre*, graal, engraving, sandblasting, acid etching, intaglio..., the list is endless.

As the skills grew in manipulating glass, so did its popularity as an object of desire. During the eighteenth and the nineteenth centuries, with the cost savings and efficiencies yielded by the Industrial Revolution, glass moved from being a prized possession of the rich to an object of everyday use. The glassmaker was no longer the artist, instead a designer would direct a team of craftsmen to manufacture the objects in the most cost-effective manner. The introduction of machines into the production line, replacing men, began the slow decline of the glassmaker's skills. In the 1960s, in the USA, glass was taken back to the artists by a potter named Harvey Littleton. He toured the art colleges of North America, inspiring the students to take up this new and yet ancient medium. This rekindled enthusiasm led to many of the old techniques being rediscovered and given a new, modern outlook. New ways of using glass are now being invented and reinvented all the time, enriching the crafts of the ancient masters.

I am often asked how long it took me to learn to blow glass. An early tutor of mine, Stan Gill, had a wonderful answer to that question. Stan, a wizened seventy-year old, used to work as a head gaffer for Stewart Crystal, arguably the leading glass manufacturer of English crystal in the twentieth century. After he had left the factory he came to my college one day a week to teach us glass-blowing skills. On this particular day he was sitting at the bench, smoking his hand-rolled cigarette with a satisfied look on his face. He had just made a flat oval dish 20cm (8in) long, with a completely even, 2cm (¾in) vertical rim all round it. It was perfect. I have never since witnessed anyone with the ability to make such an object, and I am not likely to ever again. This awestruck twenty-year-old asked Stan how long it took him to learn to blow glass and he replied, 'I'll tell you when I've learned it all.'

Glass-making is a continuous learning process. One of the joys of glass-making is the never-ending journey to master all of the techniques. The rediscovery of old and forgotten methods, combined with a modern outlook on design and colour, offers the glassmaker of the early twenty-first century a wonderful chance to create wonderful artefacts that will make future generations proud of their heritage.

CHAPTER 1

A BRIEF HISTORY
AND MODERN TIMES

Glass is one of the most common and ancient materials known to man and is present in many aspects of our everyday lives. It is used extensively in modern architectural buildings such as the Louvre in Paris and the Lloyds building in London to create stunning structural forms. Glass was also used to great effect in medieval architecture in lavishly coloured church windows to express Bible stories to illiterate congregations. Modern high-speed digital cables are made from glass fibres. These cables form the main frame of the Internet and the world-wide web which has revolutionized twenty-first-century communication. Glass has been formed into lenses to correct poor vision for hundreds of years and highly refined lenses in telescopes have helped humans look millions of miles into the sky at planets, stars and galaxies. Other lenses have helped to reveal the microscopic secrets of our own human cell structure. Greenhouses create artificial environments to propagate plants, using glass to intensify the heat and light of the sun. A glass of wine in a crystal goblet can be a perfect accompaniment to an evening meal. This versatility means that glass is also a magnificent medium for artistic expression.

When and how glass was discovered is uncertain, but there are legends and folklore about the discovery that probably still hold a grain of truth. The most widely told story is something like this:

About 4,000BC there was a merchant ship sailing up the Mediterranean carrying a cargo of nitrate. Night was beginning to draw in and so the captain decided to pull the ship over on to a beach so that the crew could light a fire and make some warm food. They made a fire out of wood and the nitrate from their cargo hold. Once the fire was roaring away they placed a large pot on top and began to cook. After filling their stomachs, they fell asleep and the fire slowly burned itself out over a period of a few hours. In the morning, among the ashes of the fire they found small, round, clear jewels in the sand. The fire had grown so hot that the sand had begun to melt. The nitrate that they had mixed with the wood for fuel had acted as a flux with the sand and tiny droplets of glass had been formed.

Glass became a highly prized substance. Recreating the environment and conditions that produced glass consistently took many hundreds of years. The earliest known glass objects are beads made in Mesopotamia about 2,500BC. These tiny objects show how great the struggle to achieve adequate temperatures for glass-making was. The development of furnace technology seems to have occurred very slowly.

The Roman era saw the greatest developments in glass-making. The innovations introduced then still form the largest body of techniques and skills used by studio glassmakers. The first hollow vessels were made by dipping: a solid shape or a mould was made and attached to a stick; the stick formed a long handle so that the glassmaker would not get badly burned by the heat of the glass and the furnace. The moulded shape at the end of the stick was plunged into the molten glass resting in a pool in the base of the furnace. Care would be taken to make sure that the mould was completely covered in glass, but it was quickly removed from the furnace before the stick had burned away. After the glass had cooled, the charred mould would be gently chipped away to leave the hollow glass form.

OPPOSITE PAGE:
Peter Layton: PARADISO VASE.

Jonathan Anderson: BOWL.

There are many problems and pitfalls associated with creating glass in this way. However, one of the problems probably led to the invention of glass-blowing as we know it today. If a mould containing some moisture is covered by dipping it into molten glass or has molten glass poured on to it, amazing things begin to happen. The moisture turns to steam and then tries to expand. Since the central mould is hard the only soft material is the sur-rounding molten glass and the expanding steam begins to inflate the glass. Many glassmakers today still use a wet stick, often known as a 'steam stick', as a way to inflate molten glass.

The next step in the evolution of glass-blowing was for the operative to use a hollow stick to hold the hot glass. He would blow down this, using his own mouth to control the degree to which the glass would inflate. Glass-blowing as we know it was developed by the Syrians in about 50BC and the basic principles that they developed are those used by studio glassmakers today.

Around AD50 one of the greatest pieces of glass known was made: the Portland Vase. The skill shown in making this is still unsurpassed today, it represents the ultimate mastery of both a blowing ability and the chemistry of glass-making. The artisans

Ed Burke: ARTEFACTS BOWLS.

abilities learned and inherited by the master glassmaker. They proclaimed the virtues of what the critics of the time called the 'fortuitous accident' that makes each piece of handmade glass unique.

A bridge between factory and studio glass was begun by the French glassmaker Emile Galle, using experimentation and exploration to create his works of art. He worked as art director, explaining his ideas to a team of skilled craftsmen who employed a variety of industrial techniques to create Galle's visions. The arrival of what we now know as 'studio glass' was brought closer by the work of the French Fauvist painter Maurice Marinot. During the 1930s he worked with molten glass direct, employing the help of a single assistant. He battled with the complexities and inherent difficulties of hot glass as a medium for artistic expression, often creating alarming and stunning objects. The American studio potter Harvey Littleton became the final link in the chain during the late 1950s and

of Victorian England regarded the Portland Vase as the epitome of classical antiquity since it utilized both hot and cold glass-making techniques; these have been mirrored in British 'cut crystal' glass-making from the late seventeenth century onwards. 'Crystal' or 'lead crystal' was invented in Britain: lead oxide was added to sand to lower the melting temperature of glass. The introduction of lead oxide to the glass 'batch' also had the effect of vastly improving its clarity. This new, clear material could be deeply cut and very highly polished with relative ease. The resulting shimmering effect was often compared to that of clusters of diamonds.

The glassmakers of Renaissance Venice used colour to a great extent. Most of the chemistry of the colouring of glass had also been worked out by the Syrians. The idea of adding small quantities of elements such as cobalt for blue, cadmium for red and iron for green dates back to ancient times. The Venetians also improved the clarity and usability of clear soda glass, creating a product known as *crystallo*; this was particularly suitable for adding extra 'bits' of hot glass from the furnace to an object that was still being blown. Many wine glasses and goblets from this period have stunning decorative work on them, all done in the hot state; by using both coloured and clear glass, it was possible to add frills, blown stems and feet, even glass animals and flowers.

These diametrically opposed styles of glass-making became the focus of much debate in the British Arts and Crafts Movement. It was argued that mass production techniques such as the division of labour used in cut crystal manufacture created a cold, hard, 'perfect' object that was devoid of life and character. By contrast, the Venetian soda tradition utilized skills and

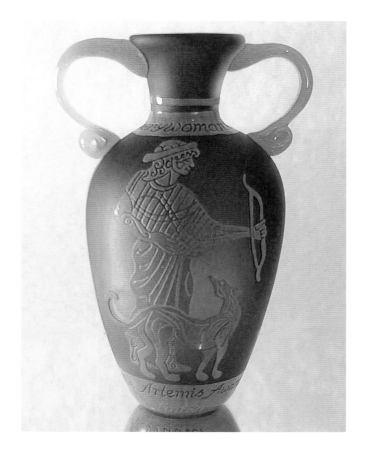

Margaret Burke: CAMEO VASE.

1960s; he had been brought up in a glass-making family and longed to be able to marry his studio pottery ideals with his glass-making heritage. He developed a revolutionary, small-scale furnace for a single artist to use instead of the huge factory furnaces that were then the only alternative. He was interested in redefining the boundaries in the manipulation of molten glass; he removed the constraints of time by working on the glass for much longer periods and would add extra coloured and clear glass as he was working. He would stretch and pull the glass to its limits, often on very large scale. The ideas of form and function in glass were being challenged. As a direct consequence of Littleton's demonstrations from his furnace a hot glass course was set up in the University of Wisconsin in 1963. This course was replicated by many other universities and colleges all over the world in the following years, which created a new breed of art graduate and, as a consequence, established the birth of the studio glass movement.

The establishment of The Glasshouse in Covent Garden in London epitomized for many the arrival of this movement in the United Kingdom. The Glasshouse was run as a co-operative organization and had many artists working in it during its life time, such as Sam Herman, Peter Layton, Charlie Meaker, Simon Moore, Steven Newell and Annette Meach. The Glasshouse structure encouraged the individuality of every artist who worked there. Numerous individual and distinctive approaches to glass were developed, which are reflected in the broad range of work being produced in Britain today.

Contemporary British Glass

There are many great and many more good artists working in Britain today. Those mentioned here have been chosen to represent the breadth of the styles of work currently being produced. New artists with innovative and bold ideas are emerging from art colleges all the time. With the arrival of new talent, more lost techniques are being rediscovered. A few hours in the many British craft galleries will confirm the importance of the current studio glass movement.

Simon Moore was heavily influenced by Memphis, an Italian post-modern design movement which influenced many glass-makers during the 1980s. The strong colour and hard angular shapes tested and stretched the makers to newer and greater heights. Moore made many large, flattened vases with spiky 'teeth' running up one edge, often with challenging colour combinations. His chandeliers and candelabra from the mid 1980s are also stunning works worthy of note. He used the

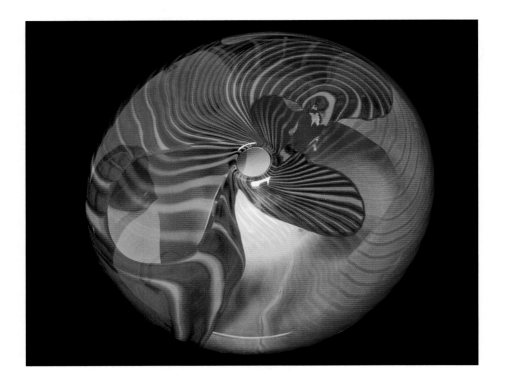

Peter Layton: PARADISO BOWL.

specialist skills gained from working with the master glassmaker Ronnie Wilkinson to take lighting sculpture to a new level.

Peter Layton, together with Sam Herman, was instrumental in setting up The Glasshouse in the early 1970s. In 1976 he set up the London Glassblowing Workshop in Rotherhithe, which moved to the Leather Market in London in 1995. He says,

> Glass is a liquid and never stops flowing – becoming sand again. As a beachcomber from way back I have attempted to capture the sun, the sea, sand and sky in my work, incorporating shell and pebble forms and lichen patterns on occasion. More recently, I have been preoccupied by ice and snow and I have sought to exploit the way glass freezes at a particular moment in the cooling process – a frozen moment, like a splash. Glass is a magical and versatile medium – man's first synthetic material.

Siddy Langley: SCENT BOTTLES.

Many people who have worked with Layton have gone on to great heights themselves. One such is Siddy Langley. She is a keen diver and underwater photographer and much of her work is influenced by the moods of the sea. She works in sympathy with the glass, allowing spontaneous reactions to the environment help to dictate the final form:

> My work tends to reflect my immediate environment. Inanimate objects, feelings and ideas are all expressed as colour and light within the glass. The spontaneity of working with hot glass was its first attraction. The material is never dull. It can be unpredictable and wilful and the finished piece is often far removed from the original concept. Although I do occasionally plan my designs on paper, more often the first rough sketches are done with the hot glass itself. The making of glass combines all the elements – earth, wind, fire and water – and, as such, seems a wholly natural process. I sometimes feel that I am no more than the catalyst bringing all these elements together for their own mysterious purpose.

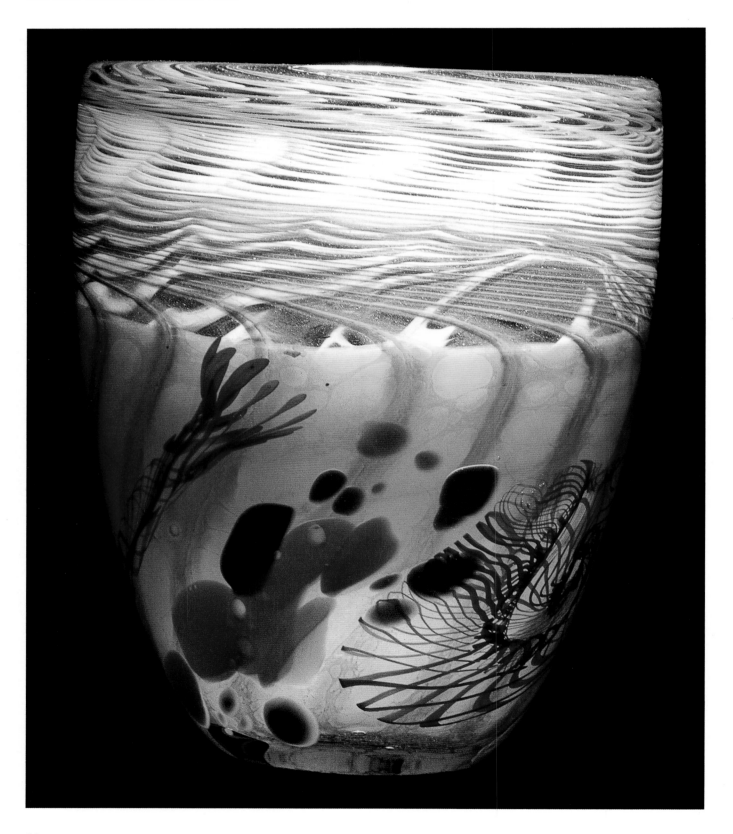

Anthony Stern is a great believer in play. He may spend days trying out new ideas, and would observe how the glass would move under various conditions; tests would be made to judge the relative movement of one colour in conjunction with another, hot glass with cold glass, and also how hot glass behaves with different metals. The tests would be done with no fixed goal in mind, keeping the emphasis on fun. The results would be allowed to seep into his subconscious and float unnoticed to the surface while making glass. In a word, the glass was allowed to evolve. Many ideas would be successful, but many would not. To Stern the road to discovery is as important as the final destination. His seascapes are stunningly bold works of pure colour. In his words:

> The inspiration for my seascapes is the English countryside. In nature there is fluid movement between the, sea, sky and rock and I aim to capture moments of this process. They are three-dimensional paintings for which glass is the ideal medium.

Catherine Hough recently won the prestigious Adrian Sassoon award at the Chelsea Crafts Fair. Her work always has strong, fluid lines and highlights the clarity of glass. She draws bold, single lines and adds faint wisps of colour to heavy, curved vase and bottle forms. These pieces are slowly cooled and then meticulously carved and polished to accentuate their shape. She says,

> The transparency of the glass is vital for creating inner life. The outer surfaces are subjected to a wide range of techniques such as grinding, carving, sandblasting and polishing, which resolves the final form and texture of the piece.

Jonathan Harris is the son of Michael Harris, the founder of both Mdina Glass in Malta and Isle of Wight Studio Glass in the U.K. He specializes in designing and producing stunningly high-quality, hand-carved cameo and *graal* glassware. Silver leaf and gold leaf are used extensively in his work. His small studio is based in the Coalport china museum in the picturesque and famed Ironbridge Gorge World Heritage Site. Harris says of his work,

OPPOSITE PAGE:
Anthony Stern: SEASCAPE.

THIS PAGE:
Jonathan Harris: CAMEO GLASS.

Julia Linstead: ENGRAVED BOWL.
PHOTO: COLIN CUTHBERT

Cameo and graal, along with multilayered, 'hot' surface decoration form the core of my technical repertoire, enabling tremendous scope for colour, shape and pattern. My first pieces of graal were produced using relatively simple patterns, which I drew by hand on to the surface of the glass and then carved through the layers of colour. I continued to develop this process, which led to the refined and detailed designs that I continue to produce today. I introduced the use of 22-carat gold and sterling silver leaf into my designs, the first collection of which was launched in 1992 in Harrods and Liberty with tremendous success.

Stephen Newell first came to international prominence by winning the Coburg Prize in 1977 for the now legendary flat jug. This has a clear or frosted body and a clear or black, flattened handle attached to it. The handle ends as a disc resting on the rim opposite the spout. In addition to his blowing skills for jugs and pitchers, he is particularly well-known for his large blown plates. The plates are generally about 60–65cm (24–26in) in diameter with a black centre and a brightly coloured rim. Then, when the plates are cold, he carves stunning Chagall-like cameo images into the surface with a sandblaster.

Julia Linstead is one of Britain's most accomplished engravers. The patterns etched into the glass by her are inspired by nature,

E+M Glass: DOODLE RANGE.

especially the flora and fauna of the Scottish Borders. She draws intensively and sketches from life until she feels that she knows the subject intimately. These 'notes' are then used to produce stylized designs which are sandblasted into the glass. She never repeats the pattern in the same way, allowing the design to evolve naturally rather than stick slavishly to a master plan.

E+M Glass combines the talents of Ed and Margaret Burke. They set up their studio in 1988 in the northern Welsh Borders. Their brightly coloured, deeply etched, fun glassware can be found all over the world. His bold use of colour combined with her eye for pattern has evolved into one of the most instantly recognizable ranges of studio glassware of our time: 'The true essence of our glass is that it makes you smile.'

TOP: BASKETS.
ABOVE: GREEN CHANDELIER.
Dale Chihuly.

American Contemporary Glass

The glass artist Dale Chihuly has the official status of 'Living Legend' in the USA. There and elsewhere his influence is enormous and his work graces the homes of many of the rich and famous and can often be seen in many prominent public places. His work, which at present is always on the grand scale, is also renowned for strong colour and bold organic shapes. A number of his huge glass baskets were used as a backdrop for one of President Clinton's State of the Union addresses. He has had many successful exhibitions, including a recent show at the Victoria and Albert Museum. One of his favourite means of showing his work to the public was evident in Venice a number of years ago: he collaborated with glassmakers from Finland, Ireland, Mexico and Italy to produce some huge glass structures, which he later suspended over the canals. The work was recorded in a book and on video with the title *Chihuly over Venice*. On a trip to Britain in the 1970s Chihuly was in an accident in which he lost an eye. As a result, he no longer makes glass himself but directs other master craftsmen to make his work. Optic moulds are used extensively in much of his work, which produce ridges on the outside surface of the glass. This technique can be seen clearly in the detailed segments of his chandeliers.

His influence is not only restricted to the strength of his work, but also stems from his part in the setting up of the Pilchuck Glass School, near Seattle in the American North-West. The school runs a number of intensive, two-week courses during the summer, and the experiences to be gained there are without parallel.

Jim Mongrain is one of the master glassmakers whom Chihuly currently uses to make his work. In contrast with the huge works that he makes for Chihuly, he is an extremely skilled goblet maker, much of his own work being heavily influenced by old Venetian stemware. The intricate designs, high technical skill and delicacy of the finished pieces are testament to Mongrain's abilities. He says,

> The challenge of becoming technically proficient in the Venetian tradition of goblet making has dominated my interest since the beginning of my career. Simplicity and functionality have become important characteristics in my most recent work. Collaborating with a variety of artists on special projects and installations has proved to be a tremendous challenge and source of inspiration.

ABOVE: **Jim Mongrain making a dragon stem goblet.**

RIGHT: **William Morris at work.**

BELOW RIGHT: **William Morris:** SCULPTURE.

During the 1980s Chihuly's main master blower was William Morris. His work simulates the remains of animal skulls, prehistoric vessels and ancient bones. The pieces look as if they have been recently excavated in an archaeological dig. The influence of indigenous North Americans and Africans is undeniable. Morris's 'treasures' are often assembled in numbers on to metal armatures to create stunning mythical sculptures. He says:

> All I do is create objects from ordinary life. The real myth is that nature subjects itself upon us every day, whether we know it or not.

When explaining his work, one of his favourite quotations is from Sir Thomas More, 'The soul requires more than ideas and ruminations. It needs objects to ally itself with.'

Watching Morris work is like watching no other glassmaker. Using a trusted team to support the hot glass, he works on the piece, standing away from the glassmaker's bench, using tools that he has made himself, and reaches inside the hollow vessel and sculpts with photographic realism. Small sections of the surface are heated with a blowtorch to allow the special tools to move the glass. Noses, eyes, ears and mouths seem to appear from nowhere before your own eyes: a master craftsman producing masterful work.

19

CHAPTER 2

THE STUDIO AND EQUIPMENT

This chapter falls into two parts; the first is descriptive and the second provides practical guidance on how you can build the more expensive items for yourself.

The Workspace

There are several important factors to bear in mind when you are choosing the building for your glass studio. You will need a fairly large amount of space to work in since there will be a number of large, hot pieces of equipment that need a substantial amount of space around them, and you will also need a large space for yourself to move in. Plenty of head room is a huge asset for a glass studio. The room can get very hot and high ceilings will help to keep the work area relatively cool. Large doors will aid ventilation and also be essential when you take delivery of large pieces of equipment. Try to find somewhere with some natural light, but not too much. Natural daylight will be easier on your eyes, but strong sunshine will make the glass appear cooler than it really is. The main tool for judging the temperature of the glass while you are working with it is your eyes, so do pay attention to the number and the size of windows in your potential workshop. Do not reject perfectly good spaces out of hand because they have too much natural light, but be prepared to install blinds or screens in the appropriate places. A solid floor, not wood, is

OPPOSITE PAGE:
Hot glass workshop in Pilchuck Glass School.

THIS PAGE:
Jim Mongrain's studio in Seattle.

'The Boat House',
Dale Chihuly's studio
in Seattle.

imperative. An unnoticed blob of hot glass on a wooden floor or a small chip of hot glass that cracks and leaps out of the 'hot bin' and you could well be looking for a new studio space after yours has burned down.

The most important factor in choosing a studio space is to find somewhere that you can relax and feel comfortable. The E+M Glass studio is set in rural Wales, overlooking a small, humpback bridge straddling a diminutive, babbling brook. Anthony Stern's studio is in a small industrial unit in Battersea, London, so that he can be near the hustle and bustle of the metropolis. The variety of studios is wide, you should visit as many different ones as you can before building your own. Take ideas of what to do from some and make note of what not to do from others. It is an individual choice, but try to find somewhere that you can unwind and relax; you will be able to produce more inspired pieces of glass and have more fun doing so in an environment that suits your own personality.

Gas Supply

A good gas supply or enough room to site a propane gas tank outside is also necessary. If you find that you have no mains gas to your building and need an external gas supply you will need to check the regulations for the siting of a bulk propane tank. Currently, you need to place a standard 2,000ltr (440gal) tank on a hard concrete or flagstone base, with no part of the tank closer than 3m (10ft) to a building wall or land boundary. Larger tanks have even more strict regulations regarding their positioning. The driver who fills your tank must be able to see his wagon and your tank from a single position and the supply hose must not pass through a building at any point. The regulations say that the tank and the supply wagon must not be more than 50m (150ft) apart when the tank is being charged. In practice, the supplier will require the tank and the wagon to be no more than 33m (100ft) apart.

Electricity Supply

You also need a three-phase electricity supply of at least 45kVA; 15kVA per phase. Three-phase electricity will make your life much easier, but a single-phase supply can be made to work while limiting you greatly as to what equipment you can install. Bear in mind that all single-phase equipment can be installed in a building that has a three-phase supply, but three-phase equipment cannot be installed into a single-phase system. Three-phase motors and heaters have their 'load' evened out across all

E+M Glass studio in North Wales.

three phases. By contrast, single-phase motors and heaters do not have their load spread. When a large, single-phase motor is switched on there will be a noticeable dimming of the building's lights, and quite probably of your neighbour's lights also. As well as being inconvenient, this is an indication of how much strain you are putting on the motor. Three-phase motors run more efficiently and under less strain than their single-phase counterparts. Their main drawback is that a small, petrol-driven generator can get you out of trouble during a power cut if you have single-phase equipment; its three-phase brother would be a serious financial investment.

Tools of the Trade

Glass-blowers use a great number of tools, many of which have not changed in shape and style for centuries. The hand tools in particular are fascinating objects that can give a museum-like feel to a studio. Some tools have been designed for a specific task; others have numerous applications. There are a number of essential and large pieces of equipment needed for glass-blowing, and by contrast these have changed in recent years. Modern technology has reduced the construction and running costs of these larger machines, making small workshops and studios viable.

Furnaces

At the heart of any glass-blowing studio is a glass melting furnace. It is in essence a very heavily insulated box capable of handling internal temperatures in excess of 1,200°C (2,200°F). The furnace runs constantly, 24hr a day for weeks, months and even years at a time. Furnaces come in many shapes and sizes, and a great deal of consideration of your own circumstances and needs must be given to choosing a glass furnace. There are three main types: a continuous melt furnace, a day tank furnace and a pot furnace.

With the *continuous melt furnace*, raw materials are put into it at one end and hot molten glass is constantly available at the other. This type is invaluable when a high production rate and shift work are necessary to meet demand for the products; it is not normally what is required for a studio.

A 'day tank' studio furnace.

The *day tank furnace* is an insulated box lined with a material capable of withstanding the corrosive nature of molten glass. Traditionally, the furnace is filled with the raw materials and the glass is melted overnight. All the molten glass produced is then used up during the day, hence the name 'day tank', and the furnace is refilled for the following day. Many glassmakers find that they can melt enough material in a tank furnace to last two or even three days. However, although there are many different types of glass that can be melted in a blowing studio, not all of them can be kept hot for two or more days without the quality deteriorating. The type of glass that you intend to use may also dictate what type of furnace you need; the lining will wear out over time and then a major rebuild will be needed. But, with good care and attention to the maintenance of the furnace, a lifespan of up to ten years is possible. A furnace used daily, five days a week, for ten or eleven months of the year would be expected to last for between three and five years: using it less will prolong the furnace life, and, as you would expect, using it more will shorten it.

A *pot furnace* is an insulated box with a free-standing crucible inside that contains the molten glass. As with the day tank, raw materials are put into the furnace and melted overnight and then used during the following day. It has a few advantages over a day tank: pot furnaces generally melt more evenly because the heat can get reach the entire crucible rather than just the top surface in a tank, and, furthermore, when the pot wears out you simply replace it with another, without having to rebuild the entire furnace. The main disadvantage is the fragility of crucibles, they are prone to damage from thermal shock and do not withstand rough treatment very well; they may crack when being warmed up for the first time and also if too great a quantity of cold raw materials is put in at one time when you are melting for the following day. Changing the crucible is a fairly simple task but it will take about a week to complete, most of the time is spent waiting for the furnace to cool down so that you can begin work and then waiting for it to warm up again once the crucible has been changed.

There are a number of manufacturers who produce furnaces for what is termed 'studio use'. The phrase 'studio glass' has now come to mean almost anything that is hand-crafted, art-based and with a small production run or consists of one-of-a-kind glass objects. By definition, a studio glass furnace would be small, with a glass capacity of between 25–300kg (50–650lb) and be quite fuel efficient. It may be gas- (bottled or natural), oil- or electrically-heated. The choice of fuel depends to a large extent upon your circumstances, but it is generally recognized that natural gas is currently the cheapest and most versatile fuel for a furnace.

RIGHT: **Small, portable glass-melting furnace in a trailer.**

BELOW: **Large glory hole at the Pilchuck Glass School.**

The 'Glory Hole'

A non-essential, but extremely useful piece of equipment is a small reheating chamber known as a 'glory hole'. It is generally used at a temperature of about 1,200°C (2,200°F) which is 100–200°C (200–400°F) hotter than the furnace's normal working temperature. The glory hole is used to speed up the process of reintroducing heat to the piece of glass that you are working on. The glory hole makes reheating easier and more accurate. It is an expensive piece of equipment to run and so a cheaper alternative is to use the mouth of the furnace. Most small studios reheat the glass at the furnace mouth in the first year or two of their existence. Using the furnace in this way does drastically reduce its efficiency and can put a cold 'skin' on to the top of the molten glass. This may not be a problem, but it can be a source of what are known as 'cords' in the glass; these are lines in the body of the glass, or sometimes on its surface, that disturb its clarity. Some artists hate them, some love them, but you do need to be aware of how they are caused and how they are eliminated. This is not their only cause but it is one that is easily overlooked once your studio is running.

The Annealing Oven

Equally as essential as the furnace is the 'annealing oven', 'lehr' or, as it is sometimes known, 'the box'. The annealing oven is used to cool the glass after it has been made. Annealing is the process of taking the strain out of a piece of glass to prevent its cracking as it cools down. The glass is held at a constant temperature, or 'soaked', at around 475°C (890°F) until the difference between the inside and the outside temperature of the object has evened out. The time required depends upon the thickness and the colour of the glass.

The temperature of the annealer is slowly allowed to fall to room temperature over a period of hours, at which point the glassware can be removed from the oven. The annealer is most commonly powered by electricity although some studios have gas-powered lehrs. Most glassmakers prefer electric annealers over gas because of their simplicity and controllability in temperature range, but again your own circumstances may dictate the choice of fuel. The temperature needed for soaking will be specific to the type of glass you use. The suppliers of the raw glass that you use can probably provide a complete temperature cycle for annealing, soaking and cooling, but if you are given only a soaking temperature, a good, average starting point is to cool the glass by reducing the temperature at 40°C (100°F) per hour. You cannot cool too slowly, but you can cool too rapidly.

ABOVE: **Glory hole at 'The Boat House'.**

RIGHT: **Lehr or annealer full of stemware at E+M Glass.**

Cooling too quickly may cause the outside of the glass to cool faster than the inside; this will induce stress in the glass and will probably cause it to crack at some point in the future.

Remember that after you have made a piece of glass it will be very hot – in the region of 500–550°C (950–1,050°F). To get your masterpiece into the annealer you will need some heat-proof safety gloves. Many studios use gloves made from a material called Kevlar. This will cope with this temperature range for a short time. The Boat House in Seattle, the studio of the great glass artist Dale Chihuly, uses safety equipment resembling an astronaut's kit to get the finished pieces into the annealer. One single piece of glass could well be worth thousands or tens of thousands of dollars so extreme care is taken with each object. Time is not too much of an issue at the Boat House Studio, but in other studios which are more speed- and production-oriented, glassmakers generally prefer to use tools that obviate any personal contact from the finished piece. Many artists have a number of homemade tools, such as planks of wood, wooden forks and various tongs adapted from barbecue sets for handling the finished objects; all the tools have long handles so that the person putting the finished object into the annealer does not have to get inside the oven. There are a few basic things to think about as you put the finished work into the annealer: when the door is opened a hot gust of air will rush out, so give yourself a second after opening the door before approaching the inside. The smell of burning hair is nearly as bad as that of burning flesh, so wear an old hat or tie your hair back from your face: no matter how short your hair is, if you are not careful, you will make it shorter when you are putting objects in the annealer. Another good tip when putting objects into the oven to cool down, is to place them on to a metal baking tray at the front of the annealer; when the tray is full it can be slid to the back of the oven with a wooden stick and another tray placed at the front again. This wonderfully simple idea was used extensively at The Glasshouse in Covent Garden in the early 1980s.

Hand Tools

It is possible for you to make your own tools. However, the savings involved are minimal, and, unless you are a skilled blacksmith and engineer, the quality is almost certainly going to be inferior. The glassmaker's bench, blowing pipes and hand tools can all be obtained easily. You should purchase hand tools and blowpipes from quality manufacturers. High-quality, handmade tools are available in most parts of the world, but there

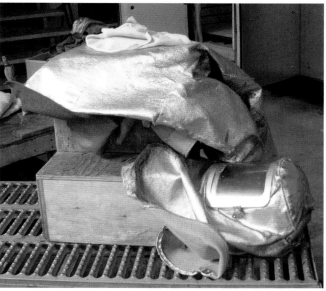

TOP: **A large bowl being put into the lehr at 'The Boat House'.**

ABOVE: **Heat-proof clothing.**

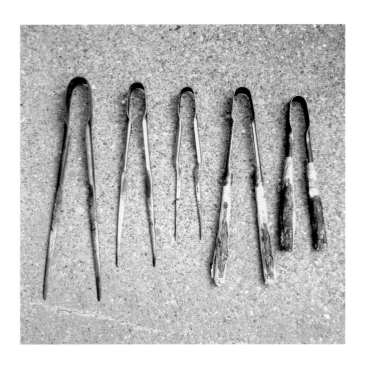

**Selection of wooden- and
metal-bladed jacks tools.**

**Straight shears, diamond
shears and rim shears.**

are many factory-produced ones that are more than adequate and substantially cheaper. One of the legendary glass tool-makers of world-wide status of the late twentieth century was Ivan Smith. He manufactured tools in a forge at the bottom of his garden. The tools were all made to measure; you could draw around your hand in pencil on a piece of paper and he would make the tools to fit the outline of it. As Smith's tools are becoming increasingly difficult to come by, a good quality alternative source is Jim Moore, based in Seattle, in the USA. He will repair old, worn or damaged tools from any manufacturer (including Ivan Smith), as well as supplying good quality tools of his own. Essemce of Sweden produce hand tools to a reasonable standard and are relatively inexpensive; their blowing irons, punty irons and foot-making tools are superb value for money. You should also note Steinart in the USA (they manufacture high-quality tools of all descriptions) and Kert Merker in Germany.

There are many hand tools designed for specific operations, many of which will be used only on rare occasions, but some are absolute necessities. The most important hand tools for the glassmaker are what is known as *'jacks'*. These are long tong-like tools that have either metal or wooden blades. The metal-bladed tools are more correctly known as *'pucellas'* and the wooden-bladed versions are called *'parchoffi'*. A good set of pucellas will be your main contact with the glass. If you are given the opportunity, try several pairs until you feel comfortable with them. They will become your best friends, the means by which you communicate with the glass, and so find a set that suits you. You can buy large, small, heavy or light and all the varieties in between, but as a general, all-purpose tool look at 20cm (8in) blades and a medium weight. With a good set of *'diamond'* shears, some *rim shears*, some medium-weight *tweezers* and some wooden-bladed jacks or 'parchoffi' there is not much that you cannot attempt to blow in glass. Choose diamond shears that will open widely; many will only open a few centimetres, especially if your hands are small. The larger the opening, the wider the piece of glass you can cut. Good quality shears are made by Cutting Edge Products of California; these are very expensive but may last over twenty-five years if treated correctly. The wooden-bladed jacks that you buy should feel as similar to your pucellas as possible; this is so that when you move from one tool to another your hands will hardly notice the difference.

The jacks are used when opening out the glassware in the final stages of manufacture; the wooden blades give a softer touch. The wood used in the jacks should for preference be from a fruit tree, cherry and pear being the best. These woods leave the fewest marks on the glass and also wear at the slowest rate. However, a famous old glassmaker, Stan Gill, from the Stewart Crystal factory in England, devised a good, cheap alternative to fruit wood; he put ordinary wooden dowelling into the jacks. He would then bind this with newspaper; the newspaper would need to be replaced every day, but its availability and low cost soon meant that most glassmakers in Britain changed to newspaper quite quickly. Kert Merker produce cardboard tubes that screw on to their own jacks and work wonderfully well. An alternative is graphite tubes; these are available from the USA, they do not mark the glass at all but do cool it down much quicker than wood, but they are also extremely fragile. Try as many variations as possible to see which suits you the best. It is also advisable to learn how to handle more than one type of jacks blade; thus, if you break graphite blades or fruit wood cannot be found anywhere, you can still use an alternative.

Blowpipes are hollow steel tubes with a mouthpiece at one end and a special, high quality stainless steel tip at the other. The tubes can be mild or stainless steel; mild steel is less liable to bend but as they age such tubes can drop annoying flakes of metal into the glass that you are working on: the stainless tubes will rarely drop metal into your glass but they are easily bent out of shape. The gathering tips may be anything from 1 to 5cm (½ to 2in) or larger in diameter for making larger or smaller objects, and are about 150cm (60in) long. Good quality blowpipes suitable for production runs and at a reasonable cost are available from Essemce in Sweden. If you intend to work on one piece for long, however, blowpipes from Steinart in the USA are probably the ones for you. At several points in the glass-blowing process, solid rods known as *punty irons* and *bit irons* are required. Stainless steel rods of 12 and 18mm (½ and ¾in) diameter, cut to lengths of about 150cm (60in) will be more than adequate for most purposes. They will wear just as well as specially tipped irons supplied by most manufacturers and are about one-sixth of the price. You can expect a life span of up to ten years from one of these steel rods. If you find that you need a punty iron that is wider than 18mm, try using a *blowing iron* instead; to use a solid iron of more than 18mm diameter would be impracticable. It would be very heavy and would soon tire you. Any imbalance because of the punty iron being too heavy also makes delicate touches while shaping the glass very difficult to carry out.

The metal tools will feel more than adequate for the delicate shaping of glass stems, handles and so on, but from time to time you will have an insatiable urge to grasp the glass with your hand and pull it into shape, but beware of the temperature of the glass – about 1,100°C (2,000°F). Do not despair

Blowpipes.

because there is a choice of two tools to overcome this yearning. Most factory glassmakers have a series of wooden '*blocks*' for the shaping of large *gathers* of molten glass. A 'block' is a cube of wood attached to a handle and will have a near hemispherical recess burned into it. These too are traditionally made from fruit trees such as cherry or pear, and need to be soaked in a water and vinegar solution for many years. If you take care of your blocks, they will last you for many years, but you will need a set of at least three differently sized ones to meet the most minimum of requirements.

A newer and more immediate solution to the need to touch glass, as we have seen, is the *newspaper*. Take a few sheets and fold them into a pad about the size of a large postcard so that it

Newspaper, copper pipe, battledore and pi dividers.

Callipers, tweezers, foot tool and 'puffer'. The puffer is used to inflate the glass when it is on the punty.

is 1 to 1.5cm (½ to ⅝in) thick. Choose a newspaper that has no colour pictures in it, if possible (for whatever reason, papers with coloured pictures in them seem to cause more ash which may stick to the glass if you are not careful), and definitely avoid using glossy magazines. Soak the newspaper in water for about 10min and then squeeze the excess of water out. Place the paper pad on the palm of your right hand; cup your right hand, and then, with your left, push the pad to the shape of your right hand. You can now take hold of the molten glass with the newspaper. You will not feel any heat from the glass through the paper for as long as you keep it wet; the pad will need to be wetted every 10 to 15sec. Keep the top surface of the pad doused in water and, after the first use or so, the smoke will diminish. You also need to keep it wet to stop little pieces of ash from sticking to the outside surface of the glass. Have an old detergent bottle filled with water at the end of your bench; this is ideal for wetting the paper pad quickly and accurately. The paper pad will burn away eventually, but, because it is cheap to replace, this is not a problem. Replace the newspaper pads at the beginning of each day; however, you should save one old pad and keep it damp for the unexpected situation. The newspaper pad will be one of the most used pieces of equipment in your studio.

Another simple tool is the *foot board*; this is the tool that is used to make feet for wine glasses. The tool may be simple but the technique is difficult to master. In its most basic form, a foot board consists of two rectangular pieces of wood joined together with a hinge. The size of the device varies according to personal taste, but two pieces about 20cm × 5cm (8in × 2in) is typical. They are hinged together along their longer edges with two pieces of leather. Many of today's glassmakers now use two plates of graphite instead of wood. Wooden foot boards will burn out of shape over time, while the modern graphite replacements will last for much longer. The technique when using graphite rather than wood is identical, but you must act faster. The graphite will cool the glass much more quickly than wood and so confidence in your abilities is a prerequisite.

Many glassmakers use a large, thick, metal plate to shape the glass. This is known as a *marver*. It consists of a perfectly flat, polished steel plate on a stand about 60–70cm (24–28in) high, which the glassmaker rolls the molten glass on, shaping and cooling it simultaneously. Marvering is a difficult technique for the beginner to master, but, once learned, is invaluable. Many of the tools used in glass-making had their origins in Italy, where a perfectly flat, thick slab of marble was used to roll glass on. According to the *Oxford English Dictionary*, 'marver' is a corrupt version of the French *marbre* (marble), but over the years the material used changed from marble to steel.

Marvering plate.

In this part of the chapter advice is given on the construction of the major pieces of equipment.

You will find that a few basic DIY skills are required, along-side patience and the enjoyment of hard work, *but you must ensure that all gas and electrical installations and connections are carried out by qualified engineers.* Safety must always be at the forefront of your mind when in a glass studio. This is just as important while you are setting up your studio as when you are using it. The careful consideration of the positioning of equipment for ease of use is essential, but you must also keep in mind your routes of escape (our local fire service chief was very helpful at this stage of the setting up of our studio). Always seek professional help and advice where you can. There are a number of glass technicians and combustion engineers who can help with the designing of major items of equipment: Mike Tuffy of MRJ Furnaces, Richard Beadman of Plowden and Thompson and Pete Howard are good sources of advice at this early stage.

More on the Furnace

The furnace is the most essential piece of equipment and upon first sight the most imposing. However, with careful planning it need not be so daunting. There are many 'studio glass' furnaces on the market all over the world and at a great range of prices, reflecting the complexity of their workings. Clever gadgetry on the furnace can really help to keep the melting of the glass consistent and reduce the running costs. However, it is when something goes wrong, which is generally on the Friday evening of a bank holiday weekend, that the simple furnaces come into their own. But whatever type of furnace you choose you will need to have at least an elementary understanding of its workings. In their basic form they are much less complicated than you might imagine.

The simplest means of melting glass is to use a gas–air mixture through a burner and burner block situated in the wall of an insulated brick box. The simplest way of mixing gas and air is to use a 'naturally aspirated' gas injector. In this system a fine stream of gas is forced through a 'jet', sucking a measurable amount of the surrounding air with it. This principle is exactly the same as in a carburettor in a car. The gas and air then form an inflammable mixture as they arrive at the burner block.

Most other gas burners will have a forced air supply to mix with the gas, provided either by a fan or a compressor, depending upon the required pressure. The advantage of these systems

A *cracking-off box* is a simple tray that is filled with loose chipped insulation material. It is the box that the finished object is tapped into before placing it into the annealing oven. The completed glass is allowed to rest in the insulation material for a few seconds while the glassmaker or his assistant puts on protective gloves in order to move the glass to the annealing oven. The most common type of chipped insulation used is *'vermiculite'*. It is often used in loft insulation and is readily available.

There are numerous manufacturers, world wide, producing glassmaker's tools so I would advise that you check out your local suppliers before you go to the expense of importing. Talk to other glass makers in your area and find out which suppliers they use.

A naturally aspirated or venturi burner.

A gas and forced air burner.

is the ease with which they may be remotely controlled; but there are obvious additional costs to be considered. The correct balance of gas and air is imperative to the efficient running of the furnace: with either too much gas or too much air the furnace will run poorly and expensively. An incorrect mixture will create glass of poor quality and will probably cause the furnace to emit some unpleasant fumes into the atmosphere.

We noted the three types of furnace earlier; we are not concerned here with the continuous melt type. Of the other two, whether the choice is for the day tank furnace or the pot or crucible type is determined by the construction of the main walls. The essential difference between the two is in how the glass is contained. Glass is a highly corrosive material and this makes the decision as to which type you use important. In a day tank the inner lining of the walls is made from sillimanite, an aluminium silicate mineral. These furnaces are very robust, but the inner wall will erode over a number of years and the furnace will eventually need a major rebuilding. A crucible furnace has a free-standing sillimanite pot that contains the glass; when this deteriorates the pot is simply removed and a new one put in its place. The pots are fragile and a great deal of care needs to be used when handling a new one and when bringing it up to the working temperature.

The final factor to take into consideration at this stage, but by no means the least important, is the type of raw material that you intend to melt. The glass that you will melt will come in one of two types; either batch or cullet. Batch is a combination of several materials such as silica sand, pot ash, soda lime and lead oxide. There are a great many combinations of these starting materials providing many types of glass: it can be designed to cool slowly so that you have longer to use it, it can be made to sparkle for crystal ware, it can be made especially tough so that it can be used for car windscreens, or it can be made highly temperature-tolerant and so be used for oven-to-table ware; and then there are fibre glass, optical glass and even a type that is used for containing nuclear waste.

You will not be able to blow with all of these different types, nor will you be able to mix them up. Each glass has its own characteristics of colour, density, refractivity, working temperature, cooling and annealing temperatures, and, most importantly, each has its own coefficient of expansion. This measures the fractional expansion of a material per degree rise in temperature. When the temperature of glass is raised from 0–300°C (32–572°F) it expands in volume. Although the expansion is very small, if it is not managed correctly it will lead to stress in the finished object which will in turn lead to cracking sooner or later. The reverse is also true. As the glass cools down between 300–0°C it will shrink. A large part of the annealing process is to control this shrinkage.

The 'linear expansion coefficient' is determined by laboratory tests on each type of glass. It is expressed in the form of a mathematical number which shows the average rise per degree Kelvin between room temperature and 300°C. The coefficient of expansion (COE) would be expressed as $98 \times 10^{-7}°K$ but this would most often be abbreviated to COE 98.

If you mix two glasses together with different coefficients of expansion to make one object, as it cools one glass will shrink more than the other and the object will crack under the strain of being pulled in different directions at the same time. The biggest concern for studio-glass makers arises when coloured glass is introduced into an object. Thankfully most coloured glass manufacturers produce coloured glass to an expansion near to 97×10^{-7} and so we have to learn only one number. Anything in the range of 95 to 100 will probably be close enough to prevent cracking but any further variation from that could spell disaster. If you do decide to mix your own, any tiny mistake in the quantities used can cause insurmountable problems.

Premixed batch can solve many of these problems, but is much more expensive than making your own. However, mixing your own batch is a hazardous job and you will need an airtight room and high quality breathing apparatus to produce it safely. Even premixed batch may be harmful to health and breathing masks and protective clothing should be worn when handling it. A few companies have started to produce batch in a pelletized form; this has a greatly reduced amount of dust with it and as such is much safer. You should still use masks and protective clothing because although the dust hazards are greatly reduced, they are not removed entirely. Phillips in the Netherlands and Glasma in Sweden both manufacture pelletized batch and both produce outstanding results; both companies should supply you with details on how to reduce the health risks associated with their products.

Pelletized batch.

Cullet.

The simplest but by far the most expensive solution to the question of raw materials is to use *cullet*. Cullet is the term used for waste glass from the production line. It may be broken or faulty glassware, or even the sweepings from the factory floor. Most factories will remelt their own cullet in combination with their own batch, which is why it is both difficult and expensive to obtain. It melts at lower temperatures than batch and does not cause the same dust problems. When you are sourcing cullet do not forget to ask about the expansion and annealing values, a cheap deal on some cullet with an expansion of 88 could turn out to be very expensive when used with coloured glass with an expansion of 98, and the finished pieces all crack.

A batch-melting furnace will have to be able to withstand temperatures in excess of 1,300°C (2,350°F) and a cullet furnace will need to cope with 1,200°C (2,200°F). This is reflected in the quality and cost of the refractory materials used to line the furnace. There are many suppliers of these around the world. Most are run by people who are only too willing to help with advice on the latest materials or on cheaper alternatives. Stuart Wright, the owner of Wrights Refractories in the Midlands, has helped to solve many furnace problems for glassmakers over the years.

Building a Day Tank Furnace

The Platform

You need to choose the position for your furnace carefully. Find somewhere that has plenty of headroom and copious amounts of room around the sides and the back; the reason for this will be very obvious the first time you need to repair anything when the furnace is at full temperature. There should also be a strong, solid, level floor since the completed furnace could easily weigh over 1 tonne (2,200lb) when full of melted glass. It is a good idea to allow an air gap underneath the furnace by building a metal platform for it to stand on. Lay a number of 'I' section girders on the floor about 15cm (6in) apart and then place a 6mm (¼in) thick, flat, metal sheet that has been cut 20cm (8in) longer than the outside wall dimensions. Ensure that this plate is laid flat with a spirit level. Pack around the girders with thin strips of metal until it is perfectly level in all directions. With this plate level the rest of the furnace construction is a much simpler job.

The Tank

The first layer of the furnace should be made of lower-grade insulation bricks, typically a GD120 brick. Your refractories' supplier will advise you on the best type available. The brick needs to be good for temperatures of up to 1,200°C (2,200°F). Most refractory companies supply bricks in a standard 22.5cm × 11.25cm × 7.5cm (9in × 4.5in × 3in) format. Place the bricks in the centre of the metal plate so that you have a square of the required outer dimensions and 11.25cm (4.5in) thick. Do not cement or bond the bricks in any way. If any of the bricks are slightly too large, rub two together to abrade them to fit. Be careful not to rub too much and make the bricks too small. The second layer is identical to the first but comprises a higher-grade insulation brick, typically GD140. These bricks are good up to 1,400°C (2,550°F). You now have a 22.5cm (9in) platform of bricks on your metal plate.

Next place the sillimanite floor tile centrally on the platform, leaving a 22.5cm (9in) gap around each side to the edge of the bricks. Be aware that these tiles are very heavy, possibly weighing 50kg (110lb), so get some help. Then put the remaining four sillimanite tiles in place to form the tank. The tank walls should be 7.5cm (3in) taller on the two sides and the back wall. With the GD140 bricks build a wall all around all four sides of the tank, placing the bricks in such a way that each

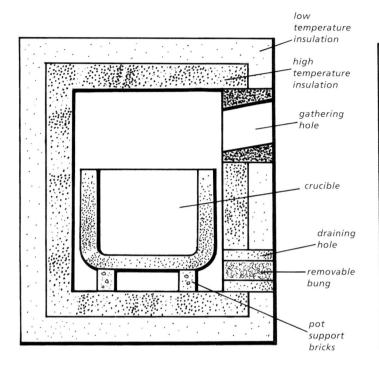

low temperature insulation

high temperature insulation

gathering hole

crucible

draining hole

removable bung

pot support bricks

Crucible or pot furnace.

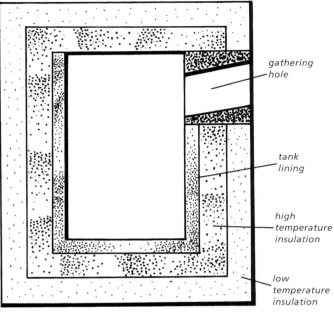

gathering hole

tank lining

high temperature insulation

low temperature insulation

Day tank furnace.

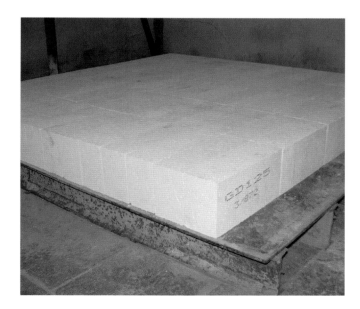

First layer of insulating bricks.

Second layer of insulating bricks.

layer is 7.5cm (3in) high. Build the wall so that it is level with the top edge of the tank and then repeat the process with GD120 bricks on the outside of the GD140 bricks. You now have a substantial structure that is around 60–70cm (24–28in) tall, with a central cavity lined with sillimanite that will eventually hold the molten glass.

The Burner Block

During the next stage the position of the burner block, the flue and the gathering hole are set and a good deal of concentration will be needed to hold these components clearly in your mind. Your burner probably will have been supplied with a cast burner block, but if it was not you should have been given instructions on how to make one for yourself, or at least the dimensions you need; but in the latter case you will find that it is a relatively easy job to cast your own burner block.

Make a solid shape out of cardboard tubes to the dimensions that you were given for the central hole. Take your time and make it as accurate as you can; the dimensions have been worked out precisely to make the burner run efficiently. Cover the tubes completely in adhesive tape so that you have an outside surface completely sealed to water. Next make a box that is open at the top and the bottom from melamine-faced chipboard; this is the material available in DIY stores for making white shelves. Screw the box together in such away that you

can dismantle it from the outside when you have finished the casting. Take another piece of faced chipboard bigger than the open ends of your box. Place your tube structure, widest tube down, on the board. Place tape round all the edges of the tube and firmly attach it to the board as neatly as you can. Make sure that no water can get between the board and the tubes. Place your box over the top of the tubes and tape it into position; again make sure that no water can escape. Put more tape on to the joints if you are unsure whether the mould is watertight. Mix castable refractory concrete capable of withstanding 1,600°C (3,000°F) such as Mizzou. There should be instructions supplied; if not, ask your supplier for help. Pour the castable concrete into your mould and tap it vigorously to make any air bubbles rise to the surface. If you were advised to make a relatively dry mixture for your particular concrete, gently pound the mixture from the open end with a wooden block to force any air out. Check how your burner is to be attached to the furnace. The most common way is for it to be bolted through four holes. Site four pieces of threaded metal bar into the half-set concrete to a depth of 5–7.5cm (2–3in). Check the position so that the threaded bars still protruding will go through the holes on the burner and that they are long enough for a nut to be put on to hold the burner in place. Cover the setting block with a plastic sheet to prevent the water from escaping too quickly and leave it for at least 24hr. Carefully remove the burner block from the mould when the castable concrete has set.

Positioning the tank lining.

Insulating around the tank.

The Gathering Hole

Making this is similar to casting a burner block. Measure the width of your furnace wall from the inside of the tank to the outside. Construct a melamine-covered, chipboard box 30cm × 30cm × [width of the furnace wall] (12in × 12in × [wall width]), leaving the top and bottom open. Construct a cardboard tube 20cm (8in) in diameter and of the same length as the wall width. Cover it with tape to make it completely watertight, attach the tube to a piece of melamine-coated chipboard with tape; make sure that no water can get between the tube and the board. Place the box centrally over the tube and tape it to the other piece of board. Mix the castable concrete as for the burner block and pour into the mould; remove the air by tapping, cover it with a plastic sheet and leave it for a minimum of 24hr. Remove the cast gathering hole from the mould when the castable concrete has set.

The Walls

Place one row of GD140 bricks on the furnace on the side where your burner and flue are going to go and then an outside

Positioning the gathering hole.

The inner casting.

layer of GD120s. Leave the top of the sillimanite completely clear for the time being. Lay the burner block on the bricks so that the back of the block, with the threaded metal bars facing out, is flush with the outside wall. The corner of the burner block on the inside should be directly in line with the inside of the sillimanite tank. On this same level place two bricks of GD120 grade, perpendicular to the others so that they protrude sideways out of the furnace. Cut another brick to 22.5cm × 7.5cm × 3.75cm (9in × 3in × 1.5in) and place it alongside the other two perpendicular bricks. You should now have a 26.75cm × 11.25cm (10.5in × 4.5in) protrusion from the wall. This is going to be the base of the flue and so it needs to be placed on the same side as the burner, but in the opposite

corner. Position the platform so that a point 7.5cm (3in) in from the platform corner is perfectly in line with the inside of the tank. Build the inner and outer walls up in the appropriate grade of brick on the two sides and back so that there are three layers above the top of the three taller tank walls. Leave a gap in the wall 11.25cm (4.5in) wide, through the inner and the outer layer, in the centre of the platform at the same height as the base of the burner block.

Place the gathering hole centrally on the front wall of the furnace, making sure that the inner and the outer face of the gathering hole are flush with the inner and the outer face of the furnace wall. Build the walls up with GD140 and GD120 bricks so that everything is level with the top of the gathering

Metal frame around the outside of the furnace.

hole. You should now be able to see into the furnace through the gathering hole, burner block and flue. Cover the inside wall above the tank with cling film, or, alternatively, you could tape bin liners into place.

The Inner Hot Face

You now need to make another wooden box from the melamine-faced chipboard, but this time open on only one side. Carefully measure the width of the inside of the tank and make the box walls to this length plus the width of the board you are using. The inside of the completed box needs to be exactly the same as the inside of the furnace tank. Make one side 30cm (12in) wide and the other three 22.5cm (9 in) wide to compensate for the shorter front tank wall. Cut one piece of board to seal one of the ends and make precise cut outs in the wooden front wall for the gathering hole block and the side wall for the burner block. Place it in the furnace, with the open end facing downwards and position it carefully over the gathering block and the burner block. Make a note of the distance between the brick wall and the wooden box. Make a wooden block measuring 11.25cm × 7.5cm × [noted measurement] (4.5in × 3in × [measurement]) and place it between the flue hole and the large wooden box. Now you need to seal the block to the box completely and both the box and the block to the cling film, making sure that everything is watertight. Stand a sealed cardboard tube 2cm (¾in) in diameter and 15cm (6in) long vertically on the top of the box; place it diagonally opposite the burner block corner and 10cm (4in) in from the edges.

Build up a further three rows of the outside wall in GD120 brick. Next construct an angle-iron frame to fit tightly round the base, the top and the four vertical walls. Use 5cm (2in) angle iron that is 6mm (¼in) thick. Weld the frame firmly into place; it will come under considerable pressure when the furnace is hot. Obtain two 'I'-section girders of the same length as the width of the furnace, and attach two high-grade, 20cm (8in) long stainless steel 'stays' to each of them; these stays should be available from your refractories' supplier. Place them on the roof, on top of the metal frame, with the stays pointing down towards the wooden box, but make sure that they are not too close to the thin cardboard tube that is protruding from the box. Cover the inside of the three top rows of brick with cling film. Mark a point on the cardboard tube 10cm (4in) up from the box. Mix a large quantity of 1,600°C (3,000°F) grade castable concrete in accordance with the manufacturer's instructions and pour it into the walls and the roof around the tube and the stays. The correct thickness of concrete is achieved when the level comes up to the mark you put on the 2cm tube. This is a large quantity of castable to handle so try to have someone to help you at this point. Tap the air free as you go. Do not stop during this particular casting until it is finished; you should immediately mix more castable if you run short. Be sure not to let any of the walls and roof part-set and then continue, such joins would probably become weak fault lines and shorten the life of your furnace. Cover the roof of the furnace with a plastic sheet to prevent the moisture from escaping too quickly after the casting is complete, and then leave it for at least 24hr to set.

The Roof

The casting for the roof must be fully dry before you continue with the furnace building. It may take longer depending on the weather that prevailed when you did the casting, but you can do no harm by waiting longer. Remove the plastic sheeting and then 100mm (4in) of 1,400°C grade, ceramic fibre blanket should be placed direct on to the cast roof. It will probably be supplied in a 25mm thick roll. Build the thickness up to four or five layers of blanket, changing the direction of the blanket on each level so as to remove any hot spots. Push each layer down firmly and make a hole in each to accommodate the ¾in cardboard tube. Change to a lower 1,200°C grade of blanket and put on another three or four layers. There are three important things to be aware of when using ceramic fibre: first, it shrinks dramatically, by up to 10 per cent, after it has been warmed up, so do not be sparing with it; secondly, it can cause much irritation and discomfort to certain skin types, so wear rubber gloves, a long-sleeved shirt and a dust mask when handling it; thirdly, and most importantly, never leave ceramic fibre uncovered after it has been exposed to high temperatures – after it has been heated up to furnace temperatures ceramic fibre is very dangerous if any dust is breathed in, but do not worry because it is easily covered (your refractories' supplier will be able to tell you of alternatives, but they will be expensive).

Fibre blanket is used extensively when building the annealer and glory holes and I shall explain how to cover it up in that situation, but to cover the roof of the furnace is easy: there should be a 25mm (1in) gap in the roof from the blanket to the girders; simply pour loose-fill vermiculite chips over the blanket and smooth them over with your hand to make it even. Vermiculite comprises small pieces of mica and is an excellent heat insulator up to about 850°C; it may be poured into many gaps that need insulating, and is often used as a loft insulator in this way; it is also available compressed into solid boards.

Build up the flue with GD120 brick to a height of at least eight layers. Space the chimney 35mm (1½in) away from the wall of the furnace then support the base of the chimney flue on an angle-iron frame that is securely welded to the furnace.

The Combustion Equipment

You are now ready to fit the gas and air pipes and it may be worth your while employing a combustion engineer to do this. Securely attach a 40cm (16in) or larger fan on a wall near to the furnace. This is not a conventional fan for cooling down a room but one produced for the sole purpose of supplying air to combustion systems. Your burner supplier will advise you or possibly even supply you with the appropriate fan. There are a number of pressure switches, taps and regulators that need to be connected between the air supply, the gas supply and the furnace burner in order to mix the gas and air correctly.

Temperature is controlled through small electronic devices that read the level inside the furnace through a sensor known as a thermocouple. The actual temperature is then compared with the temperature that you have preset into the controller; this assesses whether the temperature needs to be raised, lowered or left alone and then makes the appropriate adjustments to the gas and air supplies. Sensors and pressure switches are also incorporated into the system so that any break in the gas or electricity supply or deterioration in the flame quality will switch the system off completely such that it has to be manually restarted.

Swinging furnace door.

Sliding furnace door.

It is impracticable for me to be specific about these devices since there are many types of them. Your suppliers should be able to give you much more precise guidance. The drawings and schematics that I have included are only to show the principles involved. Each furnace needs to have its own system, tailored to its specific needs and will have its own idiosyncrasies.

Lighting the Furnace for the First Time

Connect everything up and place the thermocouple gently on its side on the roof of the furnace. Light the burner by using the main air valve and the gas valve at the back of the furnace. Set a very low temperature on the controller at around 50°C (122°F). As the thermocouple is currently situated outside the furnace, the controller will try to turn up the flame until the sensor is at 50°C. The sensor is reading the room temperature at the moment and so the temperature on the controller readout will never reach so high. You need to restrict the gas and the air supply manually down to an absolute minimum without putting out the flame; there will have been a provision for

this in the drawing given to you by your burner supplier (this provision is always made so that you can control the furnace if the controller or the thermocouple fails at a crucial time). After one hour, manually turn up the gas and the air by the tiniest amount; repeat this at hourly intervals until you can smell the wood used under the casting of the roof begin to burn then hold this setting for as long as it takes for the wood to burn away, 2 or possibly 3hr. With a small piece of copper pipe clear a path where the cardboard tube was in the roof through to the inside of the furnace; slowly and gently lower the thermocouple into the hole; do not hurry over this to avoid breaking the thermocouple sheath. There may me a blast of hot air through the hole for the thermocouple and so you may wish to wear your Kevlar gloves for this process. Leave the thermocouple to settle down for a few minutes. Next make a note of the temperature that the sensor is reading and then alter the set point on the controller to match that of the reading. You may have to do this in a number of small steps to stop the controller from overreacting to the change.

Slowly open up the manual gas and air taps over a period of from 10 to 15min. During this process the furnace temperature

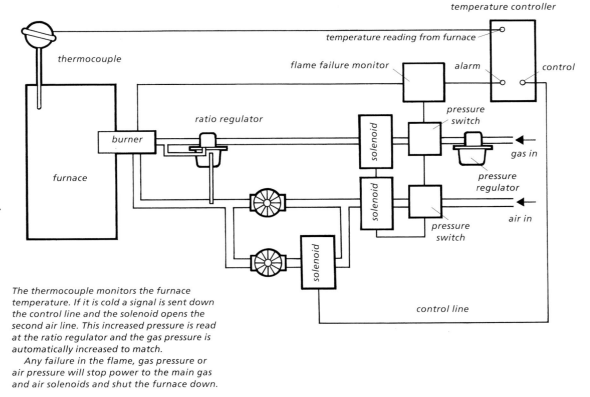

Schematic diagram for connecting power and controls to the furnace.

The thermocouple monitors the furnace temperature. If it is cold a signal is sent down the control line and the solenoid opens the second air line. This increased pressure is read at the ratio regulator and the gas pressure is automatically increased to match.

Any failure in the flame, gas pressure or air pressure will stop power to the main gas and air solenoids and shut the furnace down.

may increase wildly; if this does happen, stop and wait for it to calm down. If the temperature has not done so within 2 or 3min, turn down the gas and air until it stabilizes. Wait for half an hour and then repeat the process from resetting the control temperature. In time, you will be able to open up the gas and air taps fully without any temperature fluctuations. If there are flames or smoke around the door, reduce the gas until all the flame is contained within the furnace. At this point the controller is managing the gas and the air supply independently. You must have a ratio regulator installed to open up the gas and the air tap fully like this. But it is advisable to consult your combustion engineer at regular intervals during this initial heating of your furnace. All that you now need to do to change the temperature of the furnace is alter the set point on the controller. The set point should now be raised at a rate of 20 to 25°C (36 to 45°F) per hour until the working temperature of 1,100°C (2,000°F) has been achieved.

This whole process should take a number of days. While the furnace is warming up, the door should be made and fitted. If you are going to use the furnace as a glory hole, the door will not need to be moved often. It can be made to hook on to the metalwork on the top of the furnace, hanging down over the furnace mouth. If you are going to use a glory hole, an easily closed door will be of greater use and help greatly with fuel economy. I have seen swinging doors, hinged doors and sliding doors, each with its merits and disadvantages. Whichever mechanism you decide on, make it so that the door may be removed for repair. I have a 30cm × 30cm (12in × 12in) angle-iron frame with the connections to a swinging mechanism welded to it. I then cast into it with the same concrete with which I made the burner block. I make it about 50mm (2in) thick and then, when it is dry, I place four sheets of ceramic fibre on top and then lock the fibre in a strong metal mesh. Make sure that the handle on your door protrudes more than 20cm (8in) from the front since the heat will travel down the metal and it may become hot if it is too short. Always open the furnace door with caution.

Setting the Correct Gas and Air Mixture

When the furnace is hot the quality of the flame needs to be checked. A flame that is either too gas-rich or too air-rich will burn inefficiently and may not reach the top temperatures required. There may also be a smell of gas, the excess fuel that is not being burned up; if there is excessive gas you will see a small amount of flame or sooty smoke around the edge of the

door and/or the top of the flue. The gas should be turned down so that the flame or soot from round the door disappears. You will need to do this in order to get the furnace hot; too much gas in the mixture will make the flame too cold. Do not open the door if there is flame or soot around it since this may cause the flame to flash; this can be alarming and dangerous.

The best method of changing the flame quality is to alter the jet size on the burner: a smaller jet size setting gives a smaller hole size and therefore less gas; a larger jet size setting produces a larger hole size and so increases the volume of gas. To reduce the volume of gas by using a valve is the next best method, but the settings will need to be checked regularly, most probably weekly. There is no set formula that I know of to get the correct flame quality, only trial and error: open the door so that there is a space of say 5mm (¼in), roll up a piece of paper, light it and then put it out so that it smokes; hold the smoking paper next to the hole and note which way the smoke moves – if the smoke moves towards the furnace there is not enough air in the system and so the amount of gas needs to be reduced; if the smoke blows away from the furnace there is too much air in the system and the gas needs to be increased. Make the alterations in small increments or decrements and allow the system to settle before testing each time. The installation of a manometer on each of the gas and air lines will help you to keep the mixture in balance (a manometer is a clear plastic tube, bent into a U shape and containing liquid; the pressures exerted by the gas and the air line are reflected in the level of the liquid on either side of the U; this may be measured with a ruler and indicates the ratio between gas and air and is the key determinant when setting the mixture; your burner supplier will have told you what the recommended ratio for his equipment should be; if you wish to use a manometer ask your combustion engineer to install it on your gas train before you install the burner).

Charging the Furnace

The normal running temperature of the furnace will be around 1,100°C (2,000°F), but the exact temperature of your furnace is impossible to prejudge. The temperature shown on the controller may be 50°C hotter or cooler due to the position of the thermocouple, the type of glass you are melting and the consistency of the molten glass that you require. The melting temperatures will be around 1,200°C (2,190°F) for cullet and 1,300°C (2,370°F) for batch. The length of time that the furnace will need to be at the higher temperatures needed to melt the glass completely clear will vary with the amount put into the furnace; the more raw material, the longer it will take to 'fine out'. Eight hours is an average time for a studio furnace to melt 100kg (220lb). The process of loading the furnace with raw material is known as 'charging' and needs to be carried out in a careful but methodical manner. You should note down the times, temperatures and amounts of each charge so that any problems with the final glass quality can be traced back and improved upon next time. Many problems in glass studios creep in slowly over time; keeping a logbook of your charges will allow you to recreate a system that may have worked a number of years earlier but which you had forgotten about.

More on the Glory Hole

Which Glory Hole?

It is quite possible that the first glass you make in your own studio will be without a glory hole. When you need to reheat the glass you will simply place it in the mouth of the furnace. This is more than adequate for many jobs, but, as your ability improves, a correctly set up glory hole will become a necessary addition. It will be easier to direct the heat from the glory hole at particular parts of the glass, leaving the remainder relatively cold. A more rounded general heat and a much slower pace of work are achievable when you use the furnace to reheat the glass. The decision to use a glory hole is often an economic one; although they do not cost very much to build, they are the most expensive item in a hot glass studio to run. Unlike the furnace, you can turn the glory hole on and off as you need it, otherwise the running costs would be astronomical. A glory hole will also have an adverse effect on both the heat and the noise level in your studio.

Once you have decided to construct a glory hole the next major decision is what size to make it. This is important as it will determine the maximum size of object that you will be able to make. There are three glory hole sizes in common use in glass studios with maximum internal diameters of 20cm (8in), 30cm (12in) and 45cm (18in). The most useful, all-round size is the 30cm glory hole. You may wish to add other sizes as your needs develop. Each glory hole has its own system of doors on the front to reduce the size of the opening. When the glory hole is opened up to its maximum size either the temperature inside the hole will fall quite rapidly or the gas consumption will rise. A good system of doors to cope with this is essential.

The glory hole.

The Drum

If we assume that the 30cm diameter is the correct one for you, the first requirement is the construction of a cylindrical drum. We have determined on the diameter but consideration of the length is also necessary. A glory hole that is 60cm (24in) long on the inside will allow you to make objects up to 50cm (20in) tall. The drum will need 15cm (6in) of insulation in the walls and back to retain the heat. You need to add 30cm (12in) which is 2 × 15cm (6in) to the diameter of the hole you require and 15cm

(6in) to the length. In this case that means an outer casing of 60cm (24in) diameter and 75cm (30in) long. It is worth your time trying to find an oil drum or something similar that is close to these dimensions. If this is not possible, get a professional sheet-metal worker to construct one for you. This is an almost impossible task to do yourself and in the long run you will save much time and money by paying for a decent drum.

Lining the Drum

The drum is to be lined with 25mm (1in)-thick 1,400°C (2,500°F) grade ceramic fibre blanket. As we have seen, ceramic fibre needs to be handled with extreme care and so you must remember to wear a good face mask and rubber gloves when you are filling the drum. First, cut seven 63cm (25in) diameter circles and stand the drum up so that the open end is pointing upwards and place the circles on the bottom of the drum. At this stage the discs will be slightly too wide, but ceramic fibre shrinks dramatically when it is heated and so you need to force these seven layers into the space of six. Next you need to calculate the circumference of the drum by multiplying the diameter by the constant π (3.14); 60cm × 3.14 = 188.4cm (24in × 3.14 = 75.36in). You then add 10 per cent for the fibre shrinkage giving a total of 188.4 + 10% = 207.24cm (75.36 + 10% = 82.89in). As the blanket is 25mm (1in) thick, this means that you need to cut around about eighty-three pieces of fibre for the sides; each should be 60cm × 15cm (24in × 6in).

Stand as many pieces as you can around the inside edge of the drum; you will have many left over and will be wondering how to get them all in. There is a simple method but which requires an amount of brute force to get the fibre into the wall: get four pieces of sheet metal a little larger than the fibre strips, in this case 65cm × 20cm (26in × 8in) would be useful; put two of the pieces of metal together and slide them in-between two pieces of fibre in the wall and push them down so that there is only a little of the metal protruding inside and upwards from the fibre wall, then take a few of the remaining fibre strips and place them between the other two metal strips, making a sandwich. Ask someone to prise slightly apart the metal strips that are in the wall. Insert the metal–fibre sandwich in the gap and force it into place alongside the other fibre strips. You now have two sets of two metal strips embedded in the wall; remove one pair, leaving one set of metal plates touching each other; make another sandwich with some of the remaining fibre strips and the metal plates that you have removed and repeat the process by forcing the new sandwich between the two plates still embedded in the wall. Each time you repeat the process it will be increasingly difficult to force the fibre into the wall. To get the last piece into place you will probably need to stand on the metal plates or force it down with a hammer, or both. It is worth making this effort now otherwise, after a few months' use, you will see the fibre at the top of the glory hole sag. If this happens you will need to lay the glory hole down on its end again, force the metal plates into the wall lining and insert a few more strips of ceramic fibre to tighten it up again.

The Frame

You will need to make a stand for the glory hole. To achieve the correct height for you, ask someone to measure the height from the floor to your elbows. This should be the height of the centre of the glory hole. Construct two 'H' shapes from heavy 50mm (2in) angle iron; make the height of the 'H' the same as the floor–elbow measurement plus half the diameter of the drum. Make the crosspiece the same length as the diameter of the drum (in this instance 60cm). Weld the crosspiece at the equivalent of the diameter of the drum from the top (again, 60cm). Stand the two 'H' pieces up 75cm (30in) apart and slot the drum into the space at the top. Weld the 'H' frames to the drum so that they are in line with the front and the back.

The Burner

Make a burner block as you did for the furnace. Measure its outside dimensions and cut a hole in the drum to take the block. It should be positioned at about a quarter of the length of the outside of the drum from the front and so that the bottom of the burner block is above the centre. Having cut the hole in the metal drum, use a hacksaw blade to cut through the fibre. Place the burner block in the hole and weld a piece of angle iron between the two 'H' shapes to supply support underneath the back of the block. Now you should coat the inside of the glory hole with a mixture of firebrick cement, sand and water: take a small amount of firebrick cement and thin it down with water, add a handful of fine sand and stir well; the cement mixture will continually try to separate so stir it each time you load your brush but you will have to work quickly and boldly. When it has dried, move the glory hole to its final place and attach the burner in accordance with the manufacturer's instructions. Be sure to have any gas and electrical connections you make checked and approved by qualified engineers.

The Doors

The glory hole now needs to have a system of reducing doors or 'collars' attached to the front. I have seen many different door systems but this is the simplest system to construct: make two 25mm (1in) angle-iron square frames 40cm (16in) square, lay them on a large piece of melamine-faced board. With parcel tape, make a waterproof seal between the metal frames and the board. Make or find two cylinders, one of 22.5cm (9in) and one of 12.5cm (5in) diameter; you will probably find some old paint tins or buckets that will be adequate for this purpose – the diameters are only approximate so something close to the right size will probably do. Place one cylinder in the centre of each frame and make a waterproof seal with parcel tape. Make up

and pour some refractory castable into the frames, cover with a plastic sheet to prevent the water evaporating too quickly and leave for 24hr. Remove the cylinders from the frames and take the frames off the board; you will now have two squares of refractory castable with a circular hole in the centre of each. Obtain two pairs of gate hinges and weld the hinge-pin parts to the front 'H' frame for the door on the annealer (in the way described below at greater length), two on one side and two on the other. Make sure that the pins point upwards. Hold the frame with the larger hole placed centrally at the front of the glory hole, put two hinge arms over the hinge pins on the right-hand side and swing them so that they rest on the frame. Weld the arms on to the frame and repeat the process with the frame with the smaller hole, attaching it to the left-hand side.

Glory hole doors.

Glory hole yoke.

By carefully positioning the hinge pins you will be able to min-imize the gap between the glory hole doors and the front of the glory hole. An improvement on this system is to make each door in two pieces. Each door then opens from the left and the right; opening one half of the door then gives you an opening of intermediate size.

To change the doors to get the hole size you require simply swing the frames open and shut with an old punty iron. Be care-ful where you place the glory hole yoke; this is the name for the stand with a notch in the top that you use to rest the iron on when you are reheating. Make sure that it is either far enough back or may be moved easily so that it is not in the way of the moving glory hole doors. The half doors do not swing out as far as the full doors and so the yoke does not need to be so far back.

The yoke may be fixed or stationary and can be free of the glory hole or part of one unit. The notch where the punties or blowpipes are rested during reheating may have ball bearings in them to ease the friction when rolling the pipes. The mov-ing yokes are most often built on to 'trains' that move back and forth on rails at the front of the glory hole. Yokes of this type are extremely useful when making heavy pieces of glass.

More on the Annealer

I am sure that you will be glad to learn that an electric annealer presents fewer problems than a furnace. If three-phase electric-ity is not available to you, a single-phase annealer is possible, one that you could plug into a normal domestic power supply. A sin-gle-phase annealer would have to be relatively small and no larger than the oven in your kitchen. The principles are exactly the same as for a three-phase annealer, but with the capacity and the power requirement both reduced by two-thirds.

The lehr or annealer.

The Floor

Studio annealers are designed to sit on the floor. First make a frame from 50mm (2in) angle iron 120cm × 75cm (48in × 30in) and set it on the floor where the finished annealer is to stay. Place a row of GD120 bricks around the inside edge of the frame, resting on their 225 × 75mm (9in × 3in) face. Place the bricks so that you have bricks down one edge, turn the corner and then place three bricks. Repeat the process with another set of five and then three bricks to fill the frame. If the metal had been cut accurately, the bricks should be held tightly in place by the frame. The hole in the middle is filled with GD120 bricks, but this time lying on their 225 × 112mm (9in × 4½in) face, cutting the bricks where necessary to make sure that there are no gaps. There should still be a 35mm (1½in) recess in the centre. Fill this gap up with high temperature castable. The recess needs to be made watertight before the concrete is poured. If the bricks are left as they are they will draw water from the castable and weaken it before it has even had a chance to set. The easiest way to seal a large surface of bricks such as this is to cover it with a tough plastic sheet, such as a bin liner, in much the same way that you would line a garden pond before filling it. Cover the whole of the top surface with plastic sheeting to stop the water from evaporating from the castable too quickly after you have poured the concrete and leave it for at least 24hr.

The Walls

Cut four 112cm (45in) lengths of angle iron and weld them to each corner of the frame. The annealer looks rather like an upturned table at this stage. Now you can begin to build the walls of the annealer by placing another row of bricks on their narrow edge 9in × 3in face (225 × 75mm) on top of the already laid bricks around the outside edge. Make sure that the joints between the bricks are not above those on the previous row. This time cement the bricks into place with a wafer-thin layer of firebrick cement such as Sairset; the technique is more like glueing than cementing. The cement has no insulating properties and so needs to be kept to a minimum. Remember to leave a gap for the doorway as you begin to place the next row; it should be two bricks wide or 45cm (18in). The position of the door is important: it needs to be positioned such that no blasts of cold air can get in or hot air get out. Make it slightly stepped in from one side rather than central or dead in line with the side wall. Continue cementing

GD120 bricks in place until you have six rows with the doorway left in them, making sure that the joints are staggered from the row below.

Line the inside walls with ceramic fibre blanket after the walls have set in place. Attach it to the walls as if it were wallpaper, using the firebrick cement to hold it in place. You must remember the earlier safety instructions when you are handling ceramic fibre. The inside surface of the ceramic fibre needs to be coated when it has set in place; to do this take a small amount of firebrick cement and thin it with water, add a handful of fine sand and stir well. Brush the mixture liberally on to the fibre blanket. The cement mixture will try to separate into its constituents and so stir it each time you load your brush; you need to work quickly at this point; remember too that ceramic fibre is very porous and will instantly draw moisture from the brush.

Make your shelving for the inside of the annealer while the blanket is drying. They have two permanently fixed shelves set behind the solid walls and a movable one where the door is. The shelf frame is free-standing and is made so that it is 20mm (¾in) smaller on all sides than the inside dimensions of the annealer. Place the finished structure inside the annealer.

The Elements

Next, place the electrical elements between the shelf structure and the walls of the annealer. Use 1kW mineral-insulated elements. The main use of these is in domestic cookers; they can be coiled up and used on the hob or bent into zigzag shapes and used in the oven; they are supplied in 6ft lengths with screw connections at each end for the power source. The last 150mm (6in) at the end of each element remains cold while the middle 5ft heats up. They are electrically insulated, apart from the screw connections; for this reason, complicated switch arrangements to prevent electric shocks being received by touching the hot part of the elements are not needed; you will not get an electric shock when you put the finished glass into the lehr.

In inserting the elements you will need to bend nine of them in half to a hairpin shape. Do not make the bottom of the U bend too tight or you will fracture the element's surface. To make the bend, mark the centre of each element with a piece of chalk, place the mark over a wide piece of pipe, of about 50–75mm diameter (2–3in) and slowly bend the element around it to achieve a hairpin shape. The elements are easier to bend than you may imagine, so take your time and take care not to damage them (if your supplier will bend them to

Inside the annealer.

Mineral-insulated electrical elements.

shape for you, get him to do it). Put the elements into the annealer between the shelf frame and the wall, four across the back wall, two on either side and one in the front. Cut a piece of 50mm (2in) angle iron to a length of 60cm (24in) and place it centrally over the doorway on the inside. Cement a complete ring of GD120 bricks on top of the wall and door frame so that the walls are now eight layers high and the doorway six layers high.

The Roof

Construct an angle-iron frame, as you did for the base of the annealer, and place it on top of the wall and weld the frame to the uprights. Cut a piece of strong metal mesh to fit inside the metal frame; push the elements through the holes in the mesh from the inside of the annealer. Put a jubilee clip on the leg of each element; tighten the clips 75mm (3in) from the end so that each clip is resting on the mesh and the element hangs freely from it without touching the floor. Place a full ring of GD120 bricks around the inside edge of the frame identically with the first bricks placed in the base. Then place three 25mm (1in) layers of ceramic fibre on top of the mesh and push the elements through each layer. Make the electrical connections as shown in the diagram and then fill up the remaining space in the roof with vermiculite chips. Secure some corrugated sheeting to the top in such a way that it protects the live ends of the elements but may be removed easily when repairs are needed. Make sure that the corrugated sheeting is not close to the ends of the elements since these are electrically live and will give you a shock should you touch them or touch them with anything electrically conductive.

The Door

For the door make a metal frame 55cm × 80cm (22in × 32in) from 50mm (2in) angle iron. Cut and weld into place two pieces of flat bar 55cm (22in) long. Hold the door frame in place over the doorway and mark the position of the two pieces of flat bar on the nearest angle-iron corner upright. Separate two gate hinges, attach the hinge pins to the corner angle iron where you made the marks. Replace the long arms on the hinge pins and close them into the doorway. Hold the door frame over the doorway again and mark the position of the hinge arms on the flat bar of the door. Remove the door and attach the hinge arms to where you made marks. Fill the recess in the frame with four layers of fibre blanket. Cut some mesh to fit inside the edges of the frame but over the ceramic fibre and secure it into place; paint the exposed surfaces of the fibre with some thin Sairset, sand and water mixture and then

hang the door. There will be a small gap between the door and the wall when the door is shut of about 1–1.5cm (½in). To make the door airtight, make a piece of ceramic fibre rope 270cm (108in) long into a loop and attach it to the inside edge of the hot surface of the annealer door. To lock the door, weld a gate latch to the centre of a piece of flat bar 112cm (45in) long. Weld the bar to the top and the bottom frame on the annealer next to the closed door. Mark the position for the bar of the gate latch on the closed door and then weld it into place. Coat the exposed fibre surfaces with the cement, sand and water as before.

Using the Annealer

The running temperature will be in the region of 450–500°C (850–950°F), depending upon the type of glass you are using and on the position of the thermocouple. The exact holding temperature and the maximum rate of cooling will be obtainable from your raw glass supplier. I find that cooling at 40°C (72°F) per hour for the first 120°C (216°F), and then at 80°C (144°F) per hour works for most blown glass. A much slower rate of cooling and a much longer length of soaking will be

Schematic diagram for connecting power and controls to the lehr.

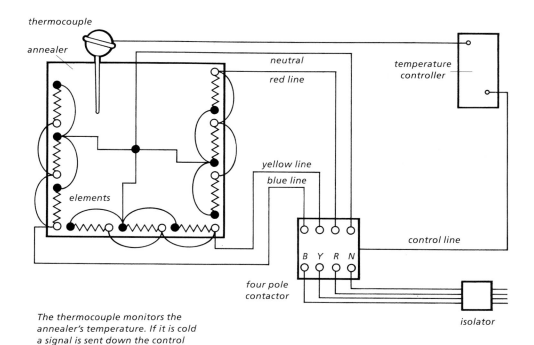

The thermocouple monitors the annealer's temperature. If it is cold a signal is sent down the control line to close the contactor allowing power to the elements.

needed when you are making particularly thick pieces of glass. It is good practice to keep an annealing log, analogous to the charging log, so that different cycles may be repeated in the future if required.

Making a Pipe Warmer

The pipe warmer is a small, insulated, open-faced box generally heated with a drilled bar burner. The pipes are rested in this to preheat them before gathering glass out of the furnace. Hot glass will not stick to cold metal easily, so the pipes are placed in the pipe warmer until the ends are glowing a dark cherry-red.

To make your own pipe warmer is an easy task: construct an angle-iron box measuring about 50cm × 30cm × 15cm (20in × 12in × 6in) from 25mm (1in) angle. Cut some thin metal sheet to line the box; cut two pieces 29cm × 14cm (11.5in × 5.5in), one piece 49cm × 14cm (19.5in × 5.5in) and two pieces 49cm × 29cm (19.5in × 11.5in). Take one of the larger sheets and cut a slot 7.5cm × 35cm (3in × 14in) 10cm (4in) in from the long side. Place the piece with the slot in it on the bottom of the box and pop rivet it into place. Similarly rivet the three sides into place, leaving the open end away from the slot. Cut two pieces of ceramic fibre blanket 50cm × 30cm (20in × 12in) and place them on the base of the box. Cement into place some GD120 bricks, standing on their 7.5cm (3in) face, to form the sides of the pipe warmer. Now put a further two

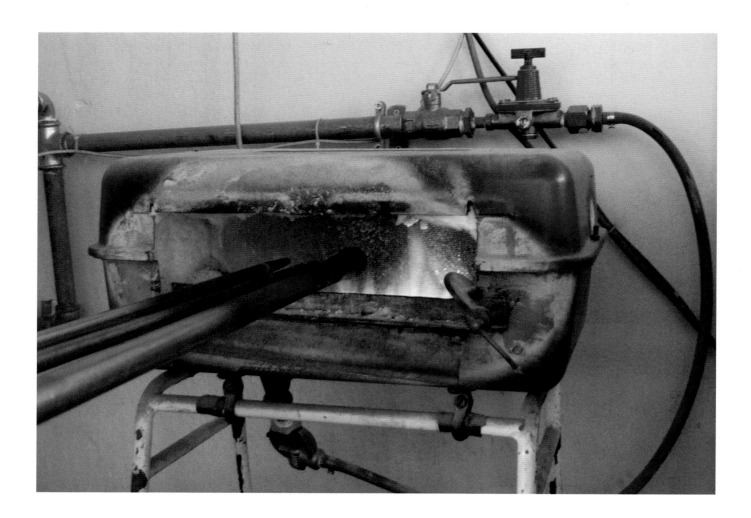

The pipe warmer.

Small venturi burner on the pipe warmer.

followed by a right-angle elbow piece; next, screw a piece of pipe 30cm (12in) long into the elbow and finish with a stop end. With a 3mm (⅛in) drill bit make three rows of thirty holes on one side of the 30cm pipe. Tighten up all the joints you have made in the pipe and then position and fix the injector and burner bar in place, just inside the slot in the base of the pipe warmer. Make sure that the series of holes are all pointing into the box. To the inlet side of the injector you need to fit a regulator and an on/off valve. A stable flame can be achieved by altering the jet size on the injector and the gas pressure at the regulator. Do not try to alter the gas pressure by partly opening the on/off valve, it will not work and is inadvisable. Ask your gas fitter to attach the pipe warmer to your mains supply in solid metal pipe, and, if this is not possible, ask him to use a high-pressure, flexible pipe. A conventional cooker hose is not suitable for high-pressure connections and it *will* burst.

Making a Glassmaker's Bench

Getting the Size Right

To construct your own bench is another straightforward undertaking. The exact shape and design of the bench is not especially important, but four specific dimensions are. First, the height of the seat needs to be considered carefully since many people make the seat too low and if the seat is not high enough you will develop back problems over time. When you sit at your bench your feet should swing freely an inch or two above the floor. Secondly, the height of the arms that the blowpipes are rolled on is critical in avoiding wrist problems such as repetitive strain injury; the ideal height of the arms would be the height of your own elbows when sat on the bench. The other two important dimensional considerations are for glassmaking reasons: the length of the arms and the size of the tool bay; be wary of making these too small as that could severely restrict your glassmaking, but if you make the tool bay too large and the arms too long, the bench may tend to tip over. The following measurements for a glassmaker's bench are for someone about 175cm (5ft 9in) tall. If you are of a very different height, measure yourself and alter the dimensions accordingly.

sheets of fibre blanket on top of the bricks and pop rivet the final piece of sheet metal into place. With a hacksaw blade cut through the fibre blanket that covers the slot on the base of the box. Attach four 60cm (24in) legs to the box, making sure that the slot is underneath.

Obtain a small, ½in venturi injector from your burner supplier. Screw a short length of ½in pipe into the end of the injector,

arm length:	90cm (36in)
arm height:	82cm (33in)
seat height:	55cm (22in)
tool bay:	30cm × 60cm (12in × 24in)

Schematic diagram for the construction of a glassmaker's bench.

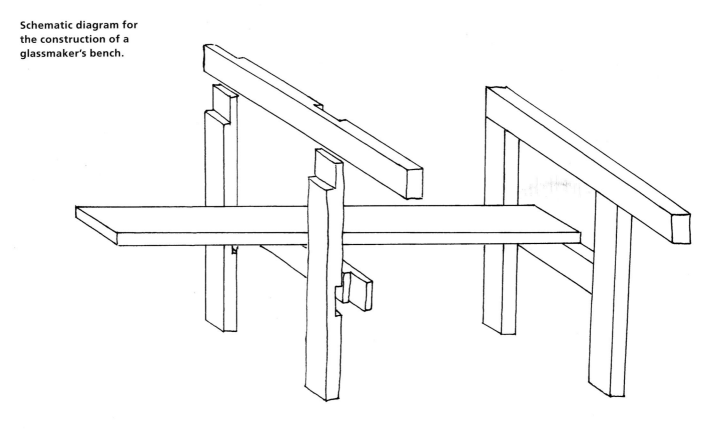

The Arms

Cut four pieces of 50mm × 75mm (2in × 3in) dressed wood to a length of 82cm (32½in). On each of these pieces cut a section away from one end 75mm × 75mm × 25mm, as shown. From the opposite end measure 50cm (20in); measure from this mark, to the non-cut end, a distance of 75mm (3in). Using these two points, measure and cut out another block 75mm × 75mm × 25mm on the same side as the first cut.

Cut two pieces of 50mm × 75mm dressed wood to a length of 55cm (22in). At each end cut away a 75mm × 75mm × 25mm block. Take one of these pieces and two of the longer pieces and put them together using the cut-outs to form an H shape. Place this on a perfectly flat surface and then glue and screw the two joints together. Repeat the process with the remaining three sections of wood. Cut two more pieces of 50mm × 75mm dressed wood to a length of 90cm (36in). At one end cut away a 75mm × 75mm × 25mm block. Measure from the cut end a distance of 55cm (22in) and then mark and cut out another 75mm × 75mm × 25mm block towards the first cut out. Repeat this on the other piece of wood. Attach each of these lengths of wood to the top of the H shapes with glue and screws.

The Seat

Next you will need a plank of wood 138cm × 20cm × 5cm (55in × 8in × 2in). Mark a line 60cm (24in) from one end and another line a further 25mm (1in) away parallel to it and then a further line another 25mm away. On the central line mark two points 50mm (2in) in from each end and drill a hole through the plank at each point. At the further point away on the plank mark two lines, one 25mm and another 50mm from the end, both parallel to the first three lines. Mark and drill two holes as you did before on the line that is 25mm from the end. Stand one of the original shapes up and slide the plank through the hole. Position it carefully between the lines 60cm (24in) from the end. With two 100mm (4in) screws attach the plank to the frame and repeat the process with the other frame at the end of the plank.

Finishing Touches

It should now look like a glassmaker's bench but you still need to do two more things to it to make it properly usable. On the right-hand arm attach a strip of metal 6mm × 5cm × 90cm (¼in × 2in × 36in). Position it so that it is raised by about 12mm (½in) down the length of the arm. On the other side lay a piece of 25mm (1in) wide draught excluder along the full length of the arm. These two little additions will greatly increase your control of the pipe when rolling it on the bench. Remember to change the strip of draught excluder every six months or so; the draught excluder will wear down without your realizing that it has happened, changing it will prevent you from losing control of the irons on the bench.

Making a Cracking-Off Box

The cracking-off box resembles a cat litter tray, it is the resting ground for the glass after you have removed it from the punty iron while you put on some gloves or pick up the appropriate tool with which to put the glass into the annealer. A good cracking-off box may be a wooden tray made from four pieces of 10cm × 2cm × 60cm (4in × ¾in × 24in) wood. The bottom is a single piece of plywood nailed on to the sides, with four 60cm (24in) wooden legs attached to the sides. Cut a single piece of ceramic fibre to fit the inside of the plywood and then fill the remaining gap with loose-fill vermiculite chips. The vermiculite needs to be changed periodically, largely because pieces of chipped and broken glass fill up the box.

Cracking-off box.

MAKING SOLID GLASS OBJECTS

Gathering

Gathering is the name that glassmakers give to the process of collecting molten glass from the furnace on the end of the blowing iron or punty iron. At first, gathering will feel like a very awkward and strange process, it may feel even a little painful until you get used to the sting of the furnace heat. To help to overcome this sting, find an old pair of socks, preferably woollen, and cut off the toes, slide one sock on each of your forearms and this will offer you quite considerable protection from the heat.

Let us look closely at your blowing iron: at one end you will notice that the blowpipe becomes a little wider; an average pipe will be about 20mm (¾in) in diameter down the length, with the last 125mm (5in) slowly increasing to 30mm (1¼in). You may be able to see where a separate section of stainless steel has been welded on here; the other end will taper off sharply to about 10mm (⅜in). The very tip may be made of plastic, brass or be a continuation of the steel. The narrow end is the mouthpiece and the wider part is the 'hot' end.

The heat and glare from the furnace can cause some eye problems over time if you do not wear the correct safety glasses.

OPPOSITE PAGE:
ELEPHANT AND SWAN.
THIS PAGE:
Preparing to gather.

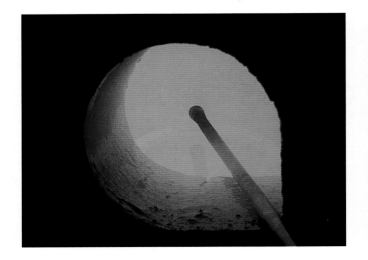

Looking for the reflection on the surface of the glass.

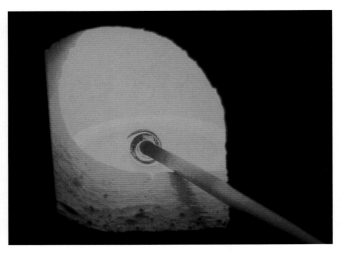

Gathering the glass.

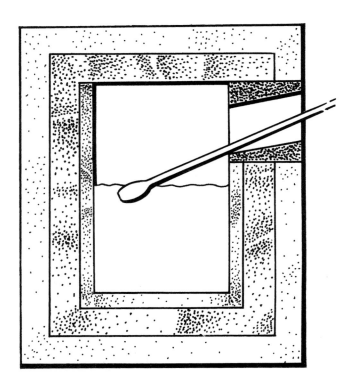

Side view of gathering glass.

You should buy glasses with lenses coated in Didymium. Didymium is a coating that can be put onto glass. It is a metallic mixture that was once thought of as an element. It is composed of 'neodymium' and 'praseodymium'. This coating reduces the harmful ultraviolet light that is emitted from the glory hole and furnace. They should not be too dark like welder's glasses because you will never be able to see what you are doing when you are away from the furnace. They can be bought with a darker band across the top which you can look through while staring into areas of more intense heat. For those of us who have to wear corrective glasses for normal use there are two solutions: you can either begin to wear contact lenses and then use normal Didymium safety glasses or ask your optician to make up some especially coated glasses to your prescription.

Rest the wide end in the pipe warmer for a few minutes. If you do not have one, put the tip of the iron into the mouth of the furnace. Allow only the last 75mm (3in) to get hot; the pipe is warm enough to use when the tip is glowing a deep cherry red colour. Be aware that the heat will travel some distance up the pipe without discolouring it; generally, the pipe will be hot for about a third to a half of its length. In order to gather some glass, begin by resting the iron horizontally in the mouth of the furnace with about 20cm (8in) of the pipe overhanging the inside wall. Move the iron over to the right-hand side of the gathering hole and gently raise the back of the iron with your right hand while you are looking at the tip of the blowpipe inside the

Taking the glass from the furnace.

furnace. Keep raising the back of the pipe until you can see a reflection of the tip in the molten glass; this reflection allows you to judge where the surface of the glass is. Push the blowing iron about 5cm (2in) into the glass, and, by using both hands, turn the pipe clockwise. You will see the molten glass beginning to be collected on the tip of the pipe. Lower the back of the pipe slightly so that the tip rises, using the gathering hole as a fulcrum. Keep turning all the time; as the pipe begins to leave the surface of the glass you will see a glass 'tail' falling from the iron into the furnace. Now increase the turning speed and most of the tail will twist back on to the pipe. This process will also make the tail become thinner and thinner and eventually snap. With the pipe still in the furnace, reduce the turning speed so that it is just enough to stop the glass from falling off the iron again. Hold the iron horizontally and the gather will begin to smooth off into a neat, round ball. Move your left hand up the pipe to about the halfway point, but before the iron gets hot, and keep

turning all the time. Rise the pipe up horizontally and remove it from the furnace. If at any point now you stop turning, the glass will fall off or at least droop to one side. Practise turning all the time so that it is an automatic process, much like breathing. The process of gathering glass should take only between 5 and 10sec to complete. The longer you spend in the furnace the further the heat will travel up the pipe, making it too uncomfortable to use. This technique is essential to the making of all blown glass and it is important to practise it.

A useful way of do this without becoming too hot and without wasting any glass is to use a bucket that is three-quarters full of water since in this way you can get used to looking for the reflection on the surface of the water and increase your speed without getting burned. (But when you are practising with water, make sure that you use only cold blowing irons.)

I repeat the need to practise gathering from the furnace; the amount of time that you practise will be shown in the ease with which you progress through the other learning stages. Before too long you will feel that you can get the same amount of glass from the furnace every time that you gather.

Safety First

When you dispose of the hot glass on blowing irons there is a simple but important routine to follow; if you do not follow this strictly somebody, someday will be burned or scalded. You need a metal garbage can and a metal bucket; fill the bucket three-quarters full with water. Place it and the bin side by side in a corner of your studio and well out of harm's way. When you wish to discard the glass, move over to the bucket of water, place your right thumb firmly over the hole in the mouthpiece of the blowing iron and immerse the pipe in water. You must keep your thumb firmly over the hole all the time that the pipe is in water. After a few seconds you will hear the glass begin to crack from the pipe and the water in the bucket will begin to boil vigorously. With your thumb still firmly in place, remove the pipe from the water and put it into the bin; only now can you take your thumb off the pipe. Try blowing down the pipe if the glass has begun to fall off to make sure that no water has travelled up the pipe. If water enters the pipe while it is hot it may instantly turn to steam and shoot out the top. Even if no steam comes out, the top will become too hot to use for some time. Nothing will go wrong as long as you keep your thumb over the end of the pipe whenever it is in water. If you ever do have water inside a blowing iron you must make everyone in the studio aware of the fact so that they do not pick up the hot iron. It is good practice to put your thumb over the end of the pipe whenever it is near water, irrespective of whether the pipe is hot or cold. It is also desirable to blow down the pipe before gathering to remove any trace of water. Make sure that you wear safety glasses whenever you are near glass that is cracking in the bin, because the glass can jump quite violently as it cools down.

Shaping the Glass

Preparation

By now your gathering ability should be coming along well, but you will feel that you want to do something else with the glass. Find an old newspaper, one that has no colour photographs in it. Place four or five sheets on top of each other and fold them in half and continue folding in half again until you end up with a thick pad about 17cm × 12cm (7in × 5in). This size is not too critical, it is more of a matter of personal taste, but make sure that it is bigger than the size of your palm with your thumb pointing sideways. Immerse the pad in water for at least 10min. After squeezing the excess of water from it, place it on the tool bay of your glassmaker's bench. Fill an empty washing-up liquid bottle with water and place it next to the newspaper pad, sit on the bench and tuck your right hip up to the right-hand arm of the bench; all your tools are to your right-hand side. All glassmakers learn to work in a right-handed manner, even the left-handed ones; this is a necessary safety rule for your workshop. With everyone having hot glass on the right-hand side of the bench there is much less opportunity for accidents to happen. It is not a handicap for left-handed people to work in this way, the fact is you need both hands all the time when you are making glass. (Anthony Stern has been one of the most successful British glass artists of the last twenty years, the fact that he is left-handed has meant that he has greater control over larger and heavier pieces than most right-handed people. His right hand soon learned to do the intricate movements needed to shape the glass in much the same way that a right-handed guitarist or violinist has to teach his left hand to finger the strings on the instrument.)

Now pick up the wet newspaper pad and place it in the palm of your right hand then with your left fist make the pad into a shallow cup the size of your right hand. Do this a couple of times to make the paper more malleable. Once the paper has been used a few times on the hot glass and really soaked it will move much better. Place the newspaper back down on the bench again.

The First Touches

Go to the furnace and gather some glass, bring the gather over to the bench, turning the iron all the time. If you stop turning, the glass is likely to fall to the floor. When you get to the bench, rest the iron on its right arm and keep turning and rolling the iron all the time. Walk round the back of the iron, continue turning, and sit down at the bench. Tuck yourself up to the right-hand arm of the bench every time that you sit at it. Keep rolling the iron up and down the bench with your left hand; roll the iron just fast enough to prevent the glass from drooping towards the floor. If you turn too fast the glass will gradually slowly spin out into a flat plate shape

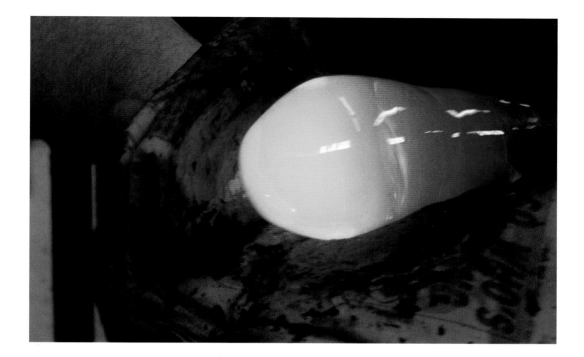

Shaping the glass with newspaper.

and will drag and drop towards the floor. Never touch the iron with your right hand when you are sat at the bench, if you do so, you will be sure to burn yourself. Pick up the newspaper pad and slightly cup the palm of your right hand with the pad in it while still turning the iron all the time. Gently place the pad under the glass and let it mould itself to the shape of the pad while still turning the glass. As you change the direction that you are rolling from up the bench to down the bench and vice versa, take the pad from the glass for a moment, this will stop the bits of ash from sticking to the glass. If you are the type of person who can pat his head with one hand while rubbing his stomach in circles with the other and can reverse the direction of the circles with ease, you will find this no problem at all. For the rest of us, I am afraid that to practise rolling up and down the bench over and over again is the only answer.

After a few seconds of use, the surface of the pad will dry out so that you will need to soak it again from the washing-up liquid bottle. Continue shaping and rolling; the first use of each pad will generally result in an enormous amount of smoke and possibly a flame coming from the pad. This is normal and not dangerous, even though it does feel rather like being burned at the stake. If there is too much smoke and flame, simply douse the pad with more water.

Reheating

At some point the glass will lose its warm glow and become too cold to move. To make the glass hot again go from your bench to the furnace or glory hole, put the glass into the heat and wait for it to warm up. Remember to keep turning it all the time. To work out how hot the glass has become is difficult; the easiest method is to count how long you have stood there reheating. When you come out of the glory hole and try to use the glass you will be able to tell whether it is soft enough to shape. If it is not, you will know that next time you need to count to a higher number. You can almost guarantee that someone will ask you a question in the middle of counting and that you will lose your place and probably cause a disaster for the glass. But after a few weeks you will not need to count and simply know when it is ready to use.

Shaping

After you have reheated it, take the glass back to the bench and repeat the shaping process. Most people tend to push too hard or squeeze too much while they are learning. You must be gentle but firm and help the glass to the required shape rather than force it. As your confidence grows, try making the glass to different shapes by using the pad alone. Try making the palm of your hand into different 'mould' shapes and see what happens; see whether you can make the glass into a wide disk and then try to make a long cylinder. Try to make some cone shapes, ball shapes, egg shapes, any shape at all, in fact. Play with the glass, experiment with it, have some fun. Do try to get most of the glass off the end of the iron and then make some different shapes. Do not worry if you fail, just have another try. You can learn as much, if not more, from something going wrong than if it goes right. Remember, ability comes from experience; experience comes from making mistakes.

Rolling the Pipe

The left hand plays a vitally important role while glass-making, especially at the glassmaker's bench. A smooth, fluid movement when you are rolling with the left hand provides a constant basis for the right hand to work on the glass. Watch other glassmakers and note what they do: some will roll the pipe from their finger tip right up their arm to the elbow; some will 'walk' the blowpipe with their finger tips, while others keep the pipe in the palm of the hand, rocking it from left to right. Watch and learn the different methods of rolling the pipe and move from one style to another regularly. Altering your technique regularly will help you to keep repetitive strain problems at bay. Pipe rolling appears to be simple but it is difficult to master; practice is the only answer, as with a child learning to walk – it will fall many times, but eventually walking will become automatic. The same can be said for many a glass-making technique, but none more so than pipe rolling.

Marvering

In addition to shaping the glass at the bench with blocks or newspaper, you can shape it on the marver. The marver is a perfectly flat, smooth, metal surface and ideal for shaping the glass when you also want it to cool rapidly. When you are standing or walking with hot glass on a blowing iron or a punty iron, always hold the pipe with the hot glass ahead of your left hand; your left hand will be somewhere near the centre of the pipe and your right hand should hold the pipe at the mouthpiece end. Approach the marver with the back of the iron lower than the height of the marver's top surface. Turn the pipe in your fingers and keep turning it as you make

contact; if you are not turning the pipe as you touch the surface of the marver you are certain to put a flat on to one side of your gather of glass. As you establish the rolling motion on the marver, use the palms of your hands to roll the iron – left palm facing down, right palm facing up – moving your hands towards and then away from each other. Bring the angle of the pipe up so that it is horizontal and parallel with the floor. Keep rolling all the time. The gather should now be mostly off the iron and have neat, round sides. To even out the tip of the gather, raise the back of the iron into the air and roll the pipe in your finger tips. Keep your hands apart on the iron when you are marvering. Try to make the transition from each phase to the next as smooth as you can. Marvering is another difficult technique to master but one well worth practising. The marver will become an increasingly useful tool as your abilities in glass-making improve.

Using the Jacks

Next you should practise using the metal-bladed jacks. This is the tool that you will use more than any other when glass-making. Marver or paper a cylinder of glass from the end of a blowing iron and take it back to the bench, and sit in your usual place at the right-hand side. Hold the jacks vertically in your right hand with the tips pointing downwards. You need to have one of the handles, just above the blade, in your fingers and the other in the palm of your hand, with your thumb coming back round to the first handle. Place the jacks around the glass and squeeze them gently. Remember to keep turning the pipe all the time. Practise making a single, neat notch in the glass. If you squeeze too hard too quickly you will flatten the glass; if the blades are slightly out of line you will end by making more than one notch or you will make a spiral. Keeping the jacks vertical as you use them and the blades parallel with the arm of the bench should avoid most of these problems. If your hand is starting to get warm, pull the bottom of the protective socks down over your palm.

When you have mastered one notch, try to make two, three and then four parallel notches. When you are reheating the glass in the glory hole or furnace, the glass that is farthest from the iron will warm up quickest. For this reason you should work from the iron end of the glass outwards. Try cutting in a notch with the jacks and then, keeping the tools squeezed together, gently push away to the right. You will see a stem-like shape being pulled from the glass. Keep experimenting and playing with new shapes, try working the glass at different temperatures,

ABOVE: **Shaping the glass with the marver.**

RIGHT: **Cutting down with the jacks.**

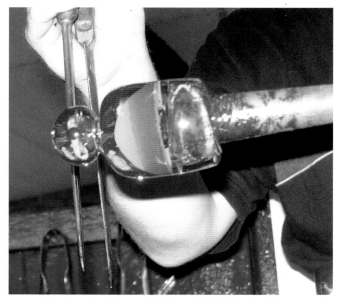

both hotter and colder. You will develop a feel for the properties of glass and this will help you enormously when you start to make objects to keep.

While you are getting to grips with the basics of hot glass-making, it is a good idea to make little glass animals and paperweights. They will help you to get a feel for the glass and how it moves and give you something to show people. Hot glass-making may be somewhat demoralizing as you learn the fundamental techniques so these items should help you to feel that you are getting somewhere.

Objects to Make

Paperweight

The simplest of all solid glass objects is the paperweight. Gather a quantity of hot glass from the furnace on a solid iron and take it to the bench, shape it lightly with the wet newspaper pad and then return to the furnace and gather more glass on top of your first gather. Make sure that your first gather is completely covered by the second. Take it back to the bench and, with the wet newspaper, drag the hot glass from the end of the iron and mould it to a round bullet shape. Reheat the glass and then, with the blades of the jacks, cut down into the glass at a point just off the end of the iron. Push the jacks away from you slightly to make a stalk about 12mm (½in) wide by 12mm (½in) long. Hold the iron vertically, with the glass uppermost, and let the paperweight settle back on to the stalk; this will have the effect of flattening the base. Move the iron back to the horizontal position and roll it up and down the bench. When the paperweight has ceased moving and cooled down, take it to the cracking-off box. Use a wooden block to tap the iron firmly about 20cm (8cm) from the hot end and the paperweight will fall into the vermiculite. Using heat-proof protective gloves, put the paperweight into the annealer. Try making paperweights of different shapes: round, flat, conical, cylindrical or whatever takes your fancy, they will be useful as Christmas presents. Try some of the colour techniques to be explained later; put the colour on to the first gather and, when it is cold enough, gather plain, clear glass over it and make the paperweight. You will be able to achieve professional-looking results quite quickly.

Elephant

Many, if not most, glass objects require a team of glassmakers. In its simplest form it is a two person team comprising of the gaffer, or chief glassmaker, and his assistant. In order to make an elephant you will need an assistant. Gather some glass from the furnace and make it into a long paperweight shape but do not cut into it with the blades of the jacks just yet. Reheat the glass, and then, with a flat-bladed tool such as a kitchen knife, make four indentations coming from the iron to halfway up the paperweight. As you push the knife in to make the first line, the glass will fall towards the floor. Turn the glass over so that it now points upwards. Make your second mark directly opposite to the first; this should have the effect of straightening the glass out. Reheat the glass and repeat the process but this time make the marks in

between the first two so that you now have a paperweight with four lines, each coming up from the iron to the halfway point on the glass. Warm up the glass again and then cut down with the jacks at the end of the iron. This cut down is the point where the completed elephant will be removed from the iron. You will probably need to go over the marks you made with the knife at this point to make them neat and even. Next, ask your assistant to bring a small blob of glass to you on a punty iron; let the hot glass fall on to the glass that you are controlling, at the top of one of the four marks; cut the blob off with the diamond shears. With the bow of the jacks flatten two sides of the blob to form a ridge in line with the knife marks. Put down the jacks and pick up the tweezers; grab hold of a small piece of the hot glass just below the ridge and pull out a length to form the trunk. When it has ceased to move, push the points of the tweezers into the flat, hot glass on either side of the ridge to form the eyes. Do not reheat it in the glory hole any more now since it will disfigure the trunk. With a wet file, saw at the cut down point at the iron and then tap the iron with a wooden block so that the glass falls into the vermiculite of the cracking-off box. While wearing heat-proof gloves, put your elephant into the annealer.

Mushroom

Gather some glass from the furnace, take it to the bench and shape it into a cylinder by using the newspaper pad. With the jacks, make the end of the cylinder into a round ball. Gently push the ball away, stretching the shape a little. Cut down with the jacks at the point where the glass meets the iron. When the glass has cooled somewhat, dip the ball back into the glass in the furnace and make a small gather. Be quick so that the cold glass does not become soft while you are still at the furnace. Make sure that you do not gather down the mushroom stalk but only on the ball at the end. Take the new gather to the bench and gently tap it flat with the bow of the jacks; pick up the footboard and place it over the flattened glass. Gently squeeze the footboard as you firmly roll the iron and the gather will turn into a disk. With the blades of the jacks make the disc into a dome by pushing the edge of the disc backwards over the stalk. You can add colour to the mushroom by using powdered and chipped colour on the marver. Make a circle about 75mm (3in) in diameter with the colour you wish the mushroom to be. Make the mushroom as above, but dip the second gather into the colour on the marver; hold it in the colour for a few seconds and then take the mushroom to the glory hole. Melt in the coloured powder and return to the bench. Use the footboard and finish the mushroom as above.

TOP: **Shaping the elephant body.**

ABOVE: **Marking the legs.**

OPPOSITE PAGE:
TOP LEFT: **Marking the legs.**

TOP RIGHT: **Cutting down at the base of the elephant.**

BOTTOM: **Adding glass for the head.**

THIS PAGE:
RIGHT: **Pulling out the trunk.**

BELOW: **The completed elephant.**

Swan

To make a swan, gather a small piece of glass and shape it to a cylinder about 35mm (1½in) long. Cut down at the iron end with the jacks and let the glass cool. Go back to the furnace and gather more glass, but only on the tip of the now cold first gather. You will need to do this quickly as the first gather will warm up and start to move if you take too long. Do not let the first gather get too cold, however, because it will crack and fall off into the furnace from the thermal shock if you are not careful. When you are back at the bench, pat the new molten glass back on to the cylindrical first gather, making a mushroom shape. With the tweezers pull a short length about 12mm (½in) out of one side of the mushroom head. Pull two slightly shorter lengths on either side of the first one. These will be the tail feathers. Roll the pipe

through 180 degrees and pull out a thin length of 35mm (1¼in) directly opposite the first three pinches; this will be the beak. With the tweezers horizontal and their tips pointing along the length of the iron, squeeze a flat piece at the base of the 35mm spike to form the head. Push the longest of the tail feathers upwards and then return to the head. Hold the head with the tweezer tips and pull the neck out to a length of 115mm (4½in) and then form it into an S shape. Speed is essential when making a swan; I have made many an ugly duckling in my time while learning how to make one. It makes a good party piece, all glassmakers like to show off, and once you have mastered the technique you will never forget how they are made. Remove the swan from the iron by using a wet file at the cut down at the base of the first gather; tap it into the cracking-off box and then place it in the annealer, while you are wearing heat-proof gloves.

THIS PAGE:
ABOVE: **Making the post for the swan.**

RIGHT: **Flattening the second gather to form the body of the swan.**

OPPOSITE PAGE:
TOP LEFT: **Pulling the tail feathers.**

TOP RIGHT: **Shaping the neck.**

BOTTOM: **The completed swan.**

Bird

Gather a quantity of glass, take it to the bench and form it to the shape of a small pear. With the jacks, cut the glass down just in front of the gathering iron. Make a small stalk about 12mm (½in) wide and 3mm (⅛in) long at the base of the 'pear'. Reheat the glass at the furnace or glory hole and return to the bench. With the tweezers, pinch a tiny piece of glass near the top of the pear shape to form the bird's beak. Turn the iron through 180 degrees and allow the glass to fall in line with the iron. Allow the

tweezers to open and then push both points into the glass on either side of the beak to form the eyes. If necessary, reheat the glass at this point – but be careful not to overheat the glass and lose the definition of the beak and eyes. Return to the bench and, again, with the tweezers, grab a reasonable amount of glass from the base of the 'pear', opposite the beak and eyes, and pull it 40–50mm (1½–2in). Point it slightly upwards; this will form the tail of the bird. With a wet file, saw the glass lightly on the stalk that you pulled at the beginning of the process and knock the glass into the cracking-off box; place it in the annealer.

THIS PAGE:
ABOVE: **Shaping the body of the bird.**

LEFT: **Cutting down the base of the bird.**

OPPOSITE PAGE:
TOP LEFT: **Pulling the beak.**

TOP RIGHT: **Poking the eyes.**

BOTTOM LEFT: **Pulling the tail.**

BOTTOM RIGHT: **The completed bird.**

CHAPTER 4

MAKING BLOWN OBJECTS

Hand-blown glassware has a very different feel from its industrial counterpart. This is mainly due to the way the glass is finished rather than how it is blown. True hand-blown glass is finished on a punty iron. You will need the help of a skilled assistant to attach a punty. Many of the techniques used in glass-making require two people, the glassmaker or 'gaffer', and the glassmaker's assistant. A small amount of glass is gathered onto the end of the punty iron and made into a punty. This is also known as a pontil. The punty is attached to the base of a blown piece to turn the glass around, this allows the glassmaker to work on the rim, using the heat of the glory hole and his tools at the bench. The mark at the base of the finished object left by the punty is often referred to as the 'signature' of a handmade piece of glass. To make a punty is a tricky craft but a very necessary one to master. A poor punty may lose its grip on a blown piece or may grip it too firmly and make a hole in the base of the finished piece. Watch other glassmakers making and using punties and notice the timing of when they use the punty and the temperature that the pieces of glass are at when the material is transferred.

Varieties of Punty

There are almost as many different types of punty as there are different objects to blow. They range from extremely lightweight ones for Venetian-style work, to huge, double-gathered ones for monumental works. There are six different types of punty explained here, but there are many others to discover as your experience increases and develops.

Italian Punty

The Italian or goblet punty is ideal for lightweight or delicate objects. It was designed for the multiple transfers required when making wine glasses in a Venetian style. Jim Mongrain uses this style of punty to make wine glasses with a magnificently sculpted dragon for the stem. This type of punty, when used correctly, will leave little or no mark at all.

Gather a tiny amount of glass on the end of the punty iron with the smallest diameter that you own. As you leave the

OPPOSITE PAGE:
E+M Glass: DOODLE VASE.

THIS PAGE:
Italian punty.

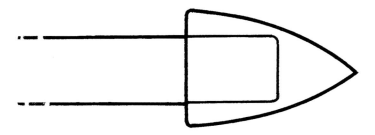

furnace, hold the iron so that the hot glass is directed towards the ceiling and starts to fall back down the iron. As this happens, move towards the marver; when there, roll the iron at a steep angle to 'point up' the remaining glass at the end of the punty. Move from this angle so that the iron is horizontal, and roll to tidy up the sides. Because there is only a small amount of glass on the end of the iron, the punty must be made very quickly. If you are slow, the temperature of the marver will chill the glass too much for it to stick to the blown object; but if you do chill the punty too much, give it a quick burst of heat in the glory hole before you present it to the gaffer. This burst of heat is often known as a flash. If everything is okay with the punty the gaffer will attach it to the base of the glass.

Alternatively, gather a small amount of glass on your smallest punty iron and go direct to the marver. Roll the iron horizontally while you pull the iron slightly towards you; this will squeeze most of the glass from the end of the iron. Then, with the diamond shears, cut as much of the glass from the end of the iron as you can. Take the half-made punty to the glory hole and warm up the glass; take the hot glass back to the marver and, at a steep angle, quickly marver the tip of the punty to a point before presenting it to the gaffer. When you have mastered this technique you will be able to use the same punty for many glasses by keeping it warm in the pipe warmer. Before reusing the punty you will need to reheat it to put some malleability back into the glass and lightly reshape the punty just before it is needed by the gaffer.

Dome Punty

This is a more substantial version of the Italian punty. Use it on slightly larger or heavier wine glasses, small vases and similar objects. Gather a small amount of glass on a small iron and hold the glass vertically upwards. As the glass falls back down the iron, walk towards the marver, start to roll on the marver at a steep angle and gradually reduce it until the iron is horizontal. You should end with an even dome of glass on the end of the iron. You may need to flash the punty over in the glory hole before you present it to the gaffer.

Doughnut Punty

The doughnut or ring punty is the workhorse in most studios; almost all joins can be made with this style of punty. The variation in the size of gather and of the iron used are relative to the size of the object being made. This punty offers a wider

diameter of contact with a blown object but with small surface area contact. This means that there will be a smaller mark left on the finished object.

Gather a small amount of glass on the end of a punty iron and hold it vertically upwards as you leave the furnace and move to the marver. Roll the glass on the marver horizontally, pulling the iron towards yourself at the same time. You should have a small amount of glass over the end of the iron. Stamp the glass-covered end of the iron on the floor or a metal plate, squashing the glass into a mushroom shape. Return to the marver and roll the glass horizontally, again pulling the iron toward yourself again to squeeze the glass to the end of the iron, thus forming a doughnut shape.

Cross Punty

This type offers a small area of contact with an object of relatively large diameter and thus is good for objects of medium to large size. If your helper is inexperienced this is a good choice of punty to use.

Ask your assistant to gather a small amount of glass on a medium-sized iron; hold the hot glass vertically upwards so that the glass creeps up the iron and then place it on the bench

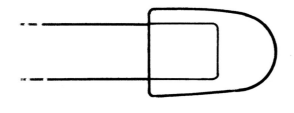

Dome punty.

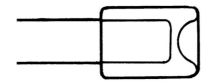

Doughnut punty.

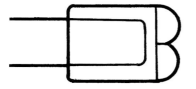

Cross punty.

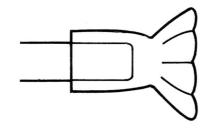
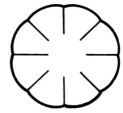

Crown punty.

for you to work on. While you make the punty your assistant should now take the blown object to the furnace or glory hole for reheating. To make the punty, use the bow of the jacks to form the glass into a dome punty and then, with the edge of the bow, cut two marks at right angles to each other into the dome to create a cross. Your assistant should now return the blown glass that he has been reheating to the bench and take the finished punty away to be attached to the base of the glass.

If you wish your assistant to make this style of punty he should use the marver. On a medium-sized iron gather a small amount of glass and hold it vertically upwards as you walk towards the marver. Make a dome punty on the marver. Hold the glass vertically upwards, resting the cold end of the iron on the floor. With a knife, make two cuts at 90 degrees to each other in the hot glass at the end of the punty to create a cross. Alternatively, the assistant can make this punty on a spare bench by using the first method.

Sand Punty

This is a variation on the dome punty. In a shallow baking tray, put a thin layer of either batch or silica sand and put it on the marver, but to one side and then make a punty as you would by the dome method. Gather a small amount of glass on a punty iron and hold it vertically upwards to let the glass fall down the side of the iron. Roll the glass on the marver, starting at a steep angle and gradually moving to the horizontal. Now, repeat the marvering process in the baking tray containing the sand. The layer of sand will prevent the punty from sticking to the bottom of the object too firmly. This means that, when it is removed, there will be scarcely any mark on

the base of the glass. This punty may be fragile and so great care must be exercised when using it.

Crown Punty

This is the large version of the doughnut punty and is thus used for very large pieces of glass.

Gather a small amount of glass on to a large iron. As you leave the furnace, hold the iron vertically to allow the hot glass to fall down the sides, as before. Move to the marver and begin to roll the glass at a steep angle then gradually lower the iron so that you are rolling horizontally to create a dome of glass at the end of the iron, again, as before. Allow the glass to cool then get a second small gather on top of the cold dome punty. This time create a large doughnut punty. To make a doughnut punty, hold the glass vertically and let it fall back down the iron. Marver the glass horizontally, pulling the iron towards you as you roll. Move quickly to the glassmaker's bench and squeeze the doughnut ring at the end of the iron with the tweezers in as many places as possible to form a 'crown'. Flash the punty in the glory hole and then present it to the gaffer.

Some glassmakers ask for the crown punty to be 'cut down' at the iron before it is attached to the glass. If this has happened, the glassmaker is not going to try to remove the punty before it goes into the annealer. In this case he will saw with a wet file at the cut-down point and detach the glass there. The remaining punty will be removed when the finished object has been cooled in the annealer, most probably by grinding the excess away on a lathe.

This by no means exhausts the range of punty types. However, I feel that, for most applications, one of these types will probably be appropriate. Each glassmaker will have his own favourites and a good assistant over time will develop an understanding with his glassmaker and know what the gaffer requires and when he needs it.

But no matter which punty type you are using, the relationship between the temperature of the blown glass and that of the punty is imperative, both need to be neither too hot nor too cold. Any deviation either way and the blown glass will fall from the punty or a huge piece of glass will be removed from the base of the blown object when the punty is removed. Often problems are caused when either the punty or the blown glass is really hot and the other is far too cold.

Problems

If you start to have problems it is necessary to step back and have a look at what is happening. Often glass will fall from the punty when on its way to be reheated for the first time. The first reaction is then generally to make the punty hotter. If it falls off again, many gaffers will ask for the punty to be made even hotter, but the glass will probably fall off yet again. The gaffer clearly needs to make a proper assessment of what is happening.

The chances are there is too great a temperature differential between the punty and the base of the blown piece. The blown object may need a quick flash to reheat the base and so reduce the difference. Making the punty hotter and hotter in this case would actually make things worse. Each problem needs to be assessed fully. Try to be aware of any extra reheats or overworking with any tools that could be altering the temperature of the glass. Also think about factors altering the punty temperature. Is the marver getting hotter? Is the iron that the punty is being made with at the same temperature as the last one? Is it wider? Is there more or less glass in the punty than before? Experience and practice, there are no substitutes.

In this second part of the chapter advice is given on how to make a number of everyday objects, applying the guidance given above.

Making a Tumbler

Before you attempt to make anything in glass you should know exactly what you are going to do, such as the shape and

E+M Glass: DOODLE TUMBLERS.

the size of the object, and there is no better way to understand the item fully than to draw it. Anyone who says that he cannot draw just needs to practise more – your drawing does not have to be a work of art, merely good enough for you and your assistant to understand the job ahead.

Getting Air into the Glass

Having decided on the shape and the size of the tumbler, gather a small amount of glass and form it to a bullet shape. While the glass is still very hot you need to put a small bubble into it. Glass has a high surface tension and thus it is difficult to get the first bubble into it. If you blow very hard, when the glass and iron are both extremely hot, you will get a bubble into the glass. With practice, a more controlled method is to apply some physics – the knowledge that hot air expands. What you should do is blow down the pipe and then quickly cover its open end with your thumb. The far end of the pipe, with the molten glass on it, is very hot; if you were successful in trapping air in the pipe, this will begin to expand. Hold your thumb tightly over the hole of the pipe so that the expanding air has only one way to grow, into the glass. This technique is not easy and requires much practice. You must keep turning the iron all the time that you are blowing and also while you are waiting for the bubble to emerge from the pipe. Try putting your thumb over the end of the pipe and then put both the pipe and your thumb into the side of your mouth, begin to blow with your thumb in place then move your thumb to reveal the hole without completely taking it off the iron. Keep blowing all the time. Put your thumb back firmly over the hole while you are still blowing, keep your thumb in place and take the pipe from your mouth so that you can watch the bubble grow. It is a useful tip to try to do this by using your other hand and thumb. You will then be able to 'thumb a bubble' from a seated position at your bench. Many people learn to do this right-handed and then try to convert to the left hand, but it is much easier in the long run to learn to use your left hand at the outset.

Blowing the Tumbler

Once the surface tension of the glass has been broken and as long as the glass is hot you can breathe gently into the pipe to expand the bubble. Try to get a spherical bubble into the bullet-shaped gather and then let it chill a little. Before the colour of the glass from the heat has completely gone, go back to the furnace and gather more glass. Make sure that all of it from your first gather is completely covered by the second one. Bring it back to the bench and shape it by using the newspaper pad as before. Blow down the pipe so that a large bubble with a wall of even thickness is on the end of the pipe. Pick up the jacks and make a neat, even cut down at the top of the bubble about 12mm (½in) from the end of the pipe. Hold the jacks vertically and use a point about 25mm (1in) from the end of the tools to mark the glass (if you have to squeeze hard, the glass will be too cold and so go back to the glory hole and reheat it); this is the point at which the glass is going to break off from the blowing iron later so make it as sharp as you can.

Take the bubble back to the glory hole and warm it all over until you can see it move slightly. Bring it out of the glory hole and hang it vertically down, keep turning all the time and start to swing it gently from side to side. The bubble will stretch into a long, cylindrical shape. As a general rule, if you find that the glass does not move much, it is too cold, but if it runs away from you out of control, it is too hot. Count how long you warm it up for on each occasion so that you can alter the length of the heating accordingly next time. If you warm only the tip of the bubble it will stretch to a conical shape, with a point at the far end. If you warm it up with the glass too far into the glory hole, it will stretch into a cone the other way round. Try to get a cylindrical shape and then take it back to the bench; by using the paper or the jacks make the sides of the cylinder smooth and straight; and make sure that you do not touch the bottom of the glass at this point, this will help it stay hotter than the rest of the tumbler. Take the glass back to the glory hole and heat it all over; if the glass is not all heated up periodically it will cool too far, crack and possibly fall off the iron. This process of heating the glass all over is known as 'flashing'. After you have flashed the glass, take it back to the bench and flatten the bottom with either a wooden paddle or the bow of the jacks. If you want the corners of the base to be well-defined and sharp, start with the paddle or jacks at a 45 degree angle and work on a corner. When the corner is established, slowly but firmly move the paddle to a 90 degree angle to flatten off the base. It is likely that the base will now be slightly wider than the rest of the tumbler and so rest the blades of the jacks down the full length of the tumbler and push the sides straight again. Remember to reheat if necessary. Taking time to reheat the glass generally speeds things up rather than slow them down. I know that it feels as if you were taking too long, but speed comes only with practice.

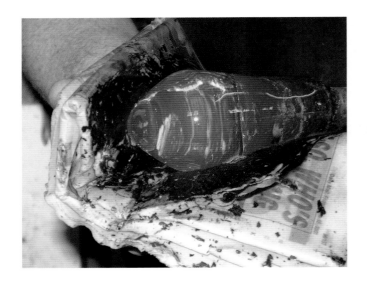

Shaping the first gather with newspaper.

Filling the tube with air.

Shaping the bubble.

Jacking down the bubble.

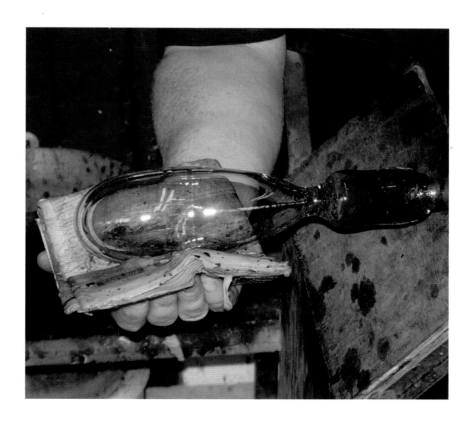

ABOVE: Swinging the bubble to lengthen it.

LEFT: Shaping the sides of the tumbler.

Transferring to a Punty

The tumbler now needs to be taken from the hollow blowing iron and transferred to a solid punty iron. The tumbler is attached so that you are then able to open out the rim. Give the tumbler a flash in the glory hole to even out the temperatures a little and then get your assistant to make a punty for you. Making a punty is not a small task and must be done with a great deal of care and attention. A bad punty may take a large piece of glass out of the final object or not even adhere to it at all if it is made badly.

We have seen the different styles of punty that are used for different jobs, but a good general purpose one is the doughnut punty. Ask your assistant to gather a small amount of glass on the end of a solid iron, dipping the iron about 12 to 20mm (½–¾in) into the glass. When he has gathered, ask him to hold the punty iron vertically so that the glass falls back down the iron slightly. He will then need to marver the sides of the glass quickly up and down so that only a small amount of glass is left at the end of the iron. Stamp the iron, glass side down, on to the floor or a metal plate for a fraction of a second, which will make the glass into a mushroom shape. Roll the sides of the glass on the marver once more, pulling the iron backwards as you roll; this will have the effect of pushing the glass forwards and you will form a doughnut of glass on the tip of the iron. To push the glass forward, pull the punty iron slightly towards you when rolling it on the marver; make sure that there is a little heat left in the glass punty, giving it a flash if necessary.

The finished punty is then brought to the glassmaker. The assistant should stand to the right of the glassmaker's bench, holding the punty iron so that the punty is close to the base of the tumbler. The position of the punty iron will mirror the position of the blowing iron. Take hold of the punty iron with the tools and attach it to the centre of the base of the tumbler; some makers use their jacks, some their tweezers and others their diamond shears, go for whatever feels comfortable to you. Once you have chosen a tool to use I would suggest that you stay with it; the consistency of using the same tool each time will give your assistant confidence. Good assistants are hard to come by so do not confuse, upset or disturb a good one by inconsistency.

Roll the blowpipe up and down the bench a few times to make sure that the join is on the centre. Your assistant will allow the punty iron to roll in their hands. The blown glass will be at the centre of the two irons with everything rotating on the same axis. Adjust the position if necessary by a series of small pushes on the punty iron with the tools. When it is central, lightly file the cut down at the rim of the glass that you

made with the jacks in the beginning. Alternatively, you may drop a tiny amount of water on the cut down or just squeeze it lightly with the jacks. After you have marked the cut down, hold the pipe firmly in your left hand and firmly tap it with the bow of the jacks. With practice, the glass will break neatly at the cut-down point and the assistant can take the tumbler on the punty, turning it all the time, to the glory hole to reheat. Take the blowpipe to the water bucket and quench the glass left on the iron. Always remember to keep your thumb over the hole when the pipe is in the water. Remove it from the water, blow down the pipe to make sure that there is no water up the iron and then put it into the bin to crack off.

Opening up the Tumbler

Now that the tumbler is attached to a punty the reheatings will become more frequent and you will also need to flash the punty joint at regular intervals. If the punty becomes too cold the tumbler will fall to the floor; if the joint is kept too warm, however, it will wobble uncontrollably and may prove difficult to remove when the glass is finished. Go to the glory hole and take over the punty iron from your assistant. Warm the top half of the tumbler up so that it is soft and moving and then bring it back to your bench, lightly run the bow of the jacks on the rim to level up any unevenness, place one blade inside the tumbler and push gently from the inside upwards and keep turning it all the time; try to allow the rim to open up to about half the required finished diameter. Work on the glass with the blade of the jacks, but be sure to work only on the surface that is below the rim. Do not touch the rim at this stage if you can possibly manage it. You will now have an enclosed shape still, but slightly less enclosed than it was before. Reheat the tumbler once more to the same degree and the same distance down the side of the glass, but this time, when you return to the bench, put both blades of the jacks inside the tumbler. By using a combination of letting the blades open under their own spring and your pushing firmly, drive the sides open to the desired position. If you do not quite get the shape that you require, warm the glass up and do it again. Try not to let the rim of the glass come out to its final position until the remainder of the glass is in place. The rim can only be made wider, it cannot be reduced. Be careful not to open the rim more than you need.

When the tumbler is finished, take it over to the cracking-off box. Rest the punty iron on the edge of the box with the glass hovering above the vermiculite. With an old dining knife, tap a few times at the point between the punty and the base of the

Flattening the base.

The punty is attached to the base.

The tumbler is taken to the glory hole on the punty.

Opening out the tumbler with the jacks.

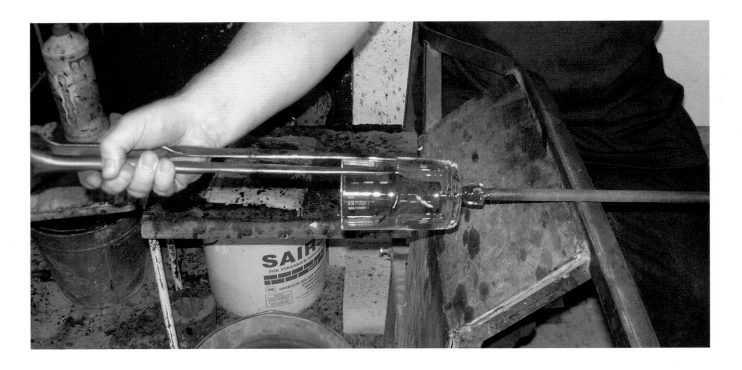

Straightening the sides.

tumbler; if the tumbler has not already come off the punty, tap the iron firmly about 30cm (12in) from the join and the tumbler will then come off. With heat-proof gloves, or whatever kind of tool you have devised, place the tumbler into the annealer.

Making a Vase

When you have mastered how to make a tumbler, blowing a glass vase should be relatively simple. It is, after all, only a large tumbler. Before making one, draw the shape that you want to make and be sure of the size that you would like it to be. Ensure that your assistant knows exactly what you are doing and what you require of him before you start.

Begin by making a small gather from the furnace, shaping it and putting a small bubble into it. Let it chill off slightly and then gather on top. Shape it with newspaper or blocks, inflate it slightly and then let it chill a little again. Gather once more and take the glass to the bench for blocking and shaping. As the size

E+M Glass: DOODLE VASE.

of the glass increases, you will need to turn the pipe more slowly. If you turn too quickly the glass will spin out into a flat disc. Work hard on the base of the vase to chill it. Use the marver to shape the glass if you feel confident. By working on the base of the gather you will create a cold spot at the end; this is needed to make the base thicker than the sides. Blow down the pipe to inflate the top of the bubble, the glass will move more at the top than at the base because the bottom of the gather is colder and therefore more viscous. Then cut the glass down with the jacks about 20mm (¾in) from the end of the iron. Reheat the glass fully and then inflate the bubble, make sure to leave plenty of weight of glass in the base; reheat the bubble in the glory hole and then swing and stretch the glass to the shape and the length that you require. As you are reheating the glass before stretching it, you need to be aware of where most of the heat is aimed; the nearer to the bottom of the bubble that you aim the heat the more pointed the base will be. The heat is aimed by altering how much of the bubble is inside the glory hole. The longer you leave the glass in the glory hole the further the base can be stretched. Again reheat the glass and take it to the bench for any final alterations, but be sure to even out the temperatures of the vase. The base will almost certainly be hotter than the top after you have stretched it.

The punty needs to be made on a larger diameter iron with a slightly larger amount of glass than was used for the tumbler so that it can take the increased weight of the vase. Attach the punty in the same way as for the tumbler; you will need to use a little more water on the cut down than you did for the tumbler to detach the blowing iron. The extent of the sawing or filing needed before knocking the glass on to the punty iron is related to the size and the thickness of the piece: thicker glass needs more chilling at the knocking-off point. Once the glass has been removed from the blowing iron, quench the blowing iron carefully in water, remembering to keep your thumb over the hole. The glass is thicker and heavier than on a tumbler and so you need to remember to turn the punty iron and the blowing iron more slowly than before. You will also need to be more patient since the glass will take longer cool down and to heat up. If you find that you cannot remove the vase from the blowing iron, remove the punty instead. Give the vase a thorough reheating at the glory hole and try again; if the vase gets too cold, especially at the rim end, it may be difficult to detach the blowing iron. Many glassmakers make the mistake of assuming that the glass is too hot when they cannot knock the object off on to the punty; the glass is generally too hot only if the blown object is still moving. Nine times out of ten the glass is too cold. In frustration, the gaffer will use

Taking a second gather.

Shaping the second gather.

Inflating the glass.

TOP: **Reheating the bottom of the vase.**

LEFT: **Swinging the vase to lengthen it.**

ABOVE: **Attaching the punty.**

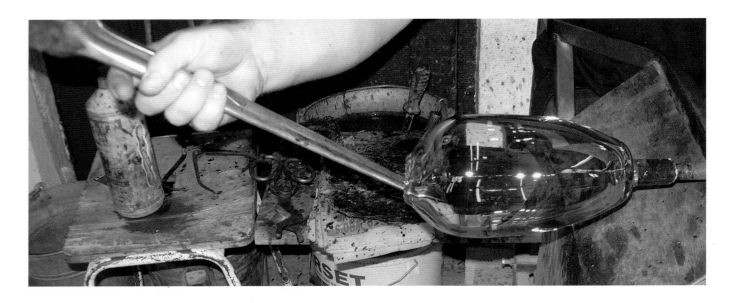

Opening out the vase with the jacks.

Opening out the vase with the newspaper.

more water and file harder as he battles to break the glass; what he is actually doing is making the glass colder and therefore making it even more difficult to remove.

Open the vase out in the same way as with the tumbler, but this time use the wooden jacks where possible instead of the metal jacks. The wooden jacks have the softer touch and so cool the glass more slowly. You can also use a newspaper pad on the outside of the vase. Remember to keep reheating the punty iron in the glory hole so that it does not become too cold and cause the vase to fall off. As you open any piece of glass you must try to leave the rim pointing inwards until the final reheating and shaping action at the bench. Once the rim has flared out it is nearly impossible to make it do anything other than flare further. If you have the sides straight and then reheat the vase, the rim will tend to flare out while you are in the glory hole. The turning action will start centrifugal forces working on the softest part of the vase and so care must be exercised when reheating. If the glass gets too hot during the reheating at the glory hole, it may also shrink in height. With practice, these two factors may be made to work for rather than against you, but, yet again, there is no substitute for practice.

Making a Bowl

To make a tall bowl blow a rounded bubble and then open it up in the same manner as you would to open up a vase. To make a shallow bowl you will need a completely different technique. Draw the shape that you want to achieve and measure the final diameter of the rim. Work out what two-thirds of the diameter is, add 20mm (¾in) to your calculation and set a pair of measuring callipers to this size. Assuming that the final diameter of the bowl is in excess of 25cm (10in), gather three times from the furnace as you did for the vase. Block and marver the glass, chilling the base as before. Inflate the top half of the bubble and cut down a cracking-off point with the jacks. Reheat the entire bubble and then, when you are back at the bench, you blow into the glass to inflate the bowl, but, at the same time, prevent the glass from moving too much at the bottom. This may be done in a number of ways: you can marver the base, making it much colder than the rest of the piece so that only the top can move. Alternatively, you can put a large wooden block or a newspaper pad on the floor, then, from a standing position, settle the bubble into the block or on to the newspaper

E+M Glass: DOODLE BOWL.

Shaping the second gather with newspaper.

Chilling the base with the marver.

Stretching the glass to thin out the rim.

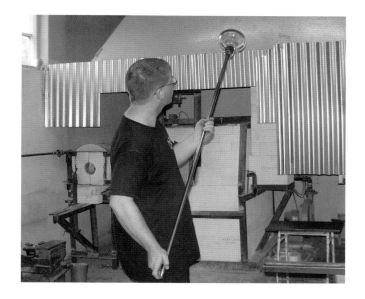

Using gravity to flatten the base.

Using newspaper to flatten the base.

Opening the bowl with newspaper.

LEFT: **Opening the bowl with the jacks.**

BELOW: **The finished bowl.**

pad. Do remember to keep turning the glass all the time. Gently blow down the pipe, the block will prevent your blowing out of the base while forcing the bubble sideways and upwards. Far easier than both of these methods is a technique that is known as a 'bench blow'; after heating the glass in the glory hole take it back to the bench and, while you use a newspaper pad on the base of the bowl, your assistant should blow down the pipe. Be clear in your instructions to your helper and choose the words you use carefully, do not use signals such as 'blow', 'slow' or 'no', which may all sound the same over the noise of the furnace and glory hole. A good assistant wants to help you to make any piece of glass to the best of your ability; be clear and definite in your instructions, for your own benefit. Let the glass inflate to the size you set on the callipers then transfer it to a punty.

The way that you reheat the glass in the glory hole is the secret to making a shallow bowl. You need to reheat deeper and to a higher temperature than you did for the vase. The glass needs to be hotter, and therefore mobile nearer to where the punty is connected than it was for either the tumbler or the vase. After the first reheat, take the bowl back to the bench and open the rim with the jacks. Try to make the bowl wider without making it any taller; if the use of the jacks makes the bowl taller, push it back down with the paper pad. Rolling the punty iron more quickly up and down the bench will help to move the sides of the bowl out and prevent it from getting taller. Keep the rim pointing inwards all the time. Before the first heat on the punty the sides of the bowl should have a slight 'S' shape towards the rim. Get the sides to a 'C' shape as soon as possible. Once this is done, reheat the bowl. Turning the punty iron quickly in the glory hole will force the sides to spin out, but take care not to spin the iron too quickly and lose the shape. Take the bowl back to the bench, keep the bowl turning quickly and you will see that the sides are starting to drift out because of centrifugal force. As this happens, use the paper pad to prevent the glass from moving too far. The pad should be held in the position that you wish the glass to have and then, by rolling quickly, the glass will be forced into the shape of the pad. Repeat the process as many times as you need to achieve the final shape. But be careful, do not try to move the glass too far. You can always reheat and move the glass again. Only on the last reheat should you let the rim point out; if you allow the rim to move out before the last reheat, you will end with a flared lip. This is true of any shape that you make, no matter whether it is a bowl, vase, tumbler or wine glass.

You will find that, with practice, the bowl will almost open up by itself. Try to reheat often without letting the bowl

E+M Glass: SORBET DISH.

become cold. Keep the glass fluid and moving all the time; you will feel in your finger tips the maximum speed at which you can turn without the glass getting out of control. If you spin the punty too quickly you will get ridges in the sides, or, in the worst case, it will spin out into a flat plate.

Making a Plate

Making a plate is very similar to making a shallow bowl. To work out the size of the bubble that you need to blow, take the final diameter that you require, halve it and add 20mm (¾in). Blow a flat bottomed bubble to this diameter and transfer the glass to a punty iron. Open the bubble up as if it were a shallow bowl until you get to the final reheat. At this point, the whole of the bubble needs to be warmed up almost to the point of collapse. Pull the punty iron back so the glass is out of the heat but stay on the glory hole yolk. Turn the iron faster and faster and the bowl will flare out into a plate. Take the plate from the punty and put it into the annealer.

This is how flat glass for windows was made in the past; small, clear pieces of glass were cut from around the edge of the plate, which is why large windows were made from many smaller panes of glass. The central piece of glass with the punty mark was known as the 'bull's eye'. This was formerly the cheapest piece of window glass but it is now by far the most expensive.

CHAPTER 5

ADVANCED STEMWARE

The reproduction of ancient stemware is an excellent method of improving your skills. Intricate stems and blown feet still have a look of quality in the modern era, but many of the original techniques have been forgotten and so some current methods, although visually appealing, are not historically correct.

OPPOSITE PAGE:
E+M Glass:
SHADOW RANGE.

Wine Glass

If there were ever one object that epitomizes the craft of glassblowing it is the wine glass. When you have perfected the many techniques needed to make stemware, there will be little that will satisfy you more as a glassmaker. Until you do perfect these techniques there will be little else that will frustrate you more. There are four distinct phases to making a wine glass, each being quite technically demanding in itself. Getting it all to come together on one piece is no small task. You

E+M Glass:
DOODLE
STEMWARE.

OPPOSITE PAGE:
TOP LEFT: **Adding the stem bit.**

TOP RIGHT: **Shaping the stem by using the jacks.**

BOTTOM: **Adding the foot bit.**

THIS PAGE:
ABOVE: **Fattening the foot bit.**

ABOVE RIGHT: **Spinning out the foot in the foot boards.**

RIGHT: **The finished goblet.**

will need a good assistant who can gather consistent 'bits', and an endless supply of patience. I shall talk you through the process as if it were all perfect the first time you attempt it. But, of course, it will not be like that, you will have to practise again and again. You may find that it is helpful to practise on each section of the glass individually, such as the stem or the foot, and then attempt to put it all together later.

Draw the shape of the glass that you want to make; always draw a new shape before you try to blow it since it will help you to clarify and understand better what it is that you are trying to do. It will also give your assistant a better understanding of what is required of him.

The Bowl

Step one is to make the bowl of the wine glass, which should not be too difficult after your having already mastered making tumblers. Gather enough glass as if you were going to make a tumbler; with practice, you will be able to get enough glass in one trip to the furnace instead of two. 'Block' the glass to shape and then 'thumb' a bubble into it. Practise using your left hand to do this; when you can thumb a bubble with your left hand you will be able to remain seated and this will save you precious time and energy, the two main enemies of a glass-blower. Cut the neck down with the jacks so that you can remove the glass from the blowpipe later, and then inflate the bubble to the size and shape that you require; with practice, you will be able to get to this stage without having to reheat at all.

The Stem

Step two is making the stem and this is where it all starts to get tricky. You now need to ask your assistant to gather what is known as a 'bit'. This is a small amount of glass, about the size of a large walnut, gathered on a spare punty iron, which may also be known as a bit iron. Gathering bits is a highly skilled job and requires much patience and practice to master. The technique is the same as gathering on a blowpipe, but the glass must be tidily held and round when you leave the furnace because neither you nor your assistant will have time to block it to shape. As your assistant moves from the furnace to the glassmaker's bench he will need to 'air marver'; he should move the glass from left to right, with the iron angled slightly down from horizontal as if rolling it on an invisible marver. As an assistant, you must learn to stop lifting the hot end of the iron up to see

whether the bit is good enough; pointing the iron upwards like that will make a perfectly good bit totally unusable.

The process of air marvering is intended to move the glass so that it is hanging from the end of the iron in a rounded teardrop shape. While your assistant is approaching the bench you should stand up inside its arms; place your left foot slightly forward and then stand your blowing iron vertically, resting the mouthpiece on top of your left foot. This is so that you do not damage the mouthpiece on the hard floor. Hold the blowpipe with your left hand and turn it through 90 degrees in both a clockwise and an anticlockwise direction while you look at the bottom of the bubble. This will help you to identify where the centre of the base of the bubble is. Pick up your diamond shears and hold them in the air, close to the base of the bubble. The assistant should stand with the bit iron in the same position as he would if he were bringing you a punty. He should then raise the iron above his head, keeping the iron horizontal all the time. The assistant should then lower his left hand, leading the glass towards the base of the wine glass; at this point the glass-maker grasps the end of the assistant's iron with the tip of the shears. This will prevent the assistant from turning the iron, so that the glass will fall off the end, to the bottom of the bubble. As the hot glass touches the bowl, turn the blowing iron with your left hand a quarter turn in each direction to make sure that you have placed the glass on centre. Release the assistant's iron from the tip of the shears and then cut the glass at its narrowest point with the blades of the diamond shears.

The assistant should now move away from this position to dispose of the glass on the bit iron. It is a good idea to keep waste clear glass in a separate bucket so that you can recycle it next time you melt glass. As your assistant moves away, you should return the glass to the horizontal position on the arms of the bench and sit down. The end of the stem bit will have a cold 'V'-shaped mark on it from the shear blades. With the bow of the jacks, quickly tap the 'V'-shaped mark into the hot glass behind it. The hot glass will then melt the mark away. For this to be effective you need to tap it once only and then not touch the sheared part of the bit until the mark has gone. While the mark is melting, move the bow of the jacks to the sides of the bit and form it into a short, wide cylinder. Cut down with the jacks about 3mm (⅛in) from the base of the bowl. Now is a good time to reheat the wine glass at the glory hole. When you are reheating at this point, your main concern should be to prevent the cold glass in the wine glass bowl from cracking. Return to the bench and make another cut down with the jacks about 12mm (½in) from the other end of the stem. With the blades of the jacks, shape the stem so that it resembles two balls, one large near the bowl and the other, a smaller one, at the end of the stem.

THE STRAIGHT STEM

If you wish to make a straight stem, you would tap the shear mark and make a cylinder exactly as before. Again, you would cut down just away from the base of the bowl, but then you should angle the jacks gently from the cut down to the base of the stem to form a small cone, with its widest part at the base of the stem. Reheat the stem and the glass and return to the bench. Lay the blades of the jacks on either side of the cone and then gently push the stem to the length that you require. It will take a great deal of practice to get the stems straight and even. With this stem shape and the previous stem shape mastered you should be able to adapt your techniques to make almost any stem shape you could wish for. Intricate stem shapes with many different thicknesses and angles may well be made from more than one bit.

FEATHER TWIST STEM

An easy way to imitate an eighteenth-century feather twist stem requires a small pad of powdered, coloured glass. Choose an appropriate colour, such as white, and make a small, round pad of colour on the marver; make the pad about 5cm (2in) in diameter. Gather enough glass for a large stem and marver the sides of the bit as if you were making a wide handle. When the sides have chilled, dip the warm end of the bit into the coloured powder. Reheat the bit in the glory hole and then dip the bit into the colour again. Warm the whole bit up in the glory hole and marver the sides on your way to the bench. At the bench, hold the bit iron still for a second and allow the bit to droop downwards. Turn the iron through 180 degrees, and, as the bit falls back, take a table knife and push it through the coloured glass until the knife touches the bit iron. Take the bit to the marver and marver the sides of the bit again. You will now have a flat band of colour that travels up the inside of the bit. The end of the bit will be a little ragged and so reheat it until it is hot and then cut off the end with diamond shears. The bit may now be cast on to the bottom of the wine glass bowl as usual. Draw the bit to the shape of the stem, but work on the bit only when you roll the iron away from you. As you get to the end of the bench, release the stem from the jacks until you roll the iron fully back down the bench. Work on the stem again, rolling the iron away from you. By working on the glass in only one direction, you will twist the feather of colour inside the stem. You

may need to grip the end of the stem more firmly to get the required amount of twist and in this case you may need to cut the end of the stem off when you have finished. You can then cast on a spun foot or a blown foot and complete the glass.

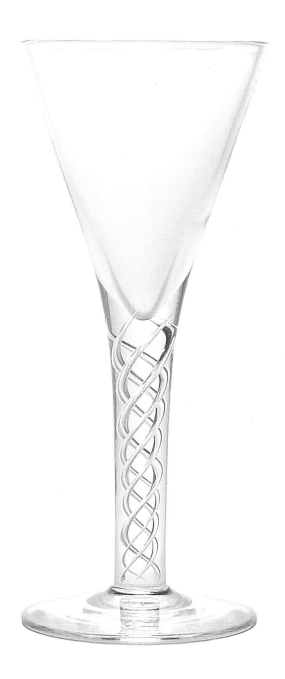

Anthony Wassell: AIR TWIST STEM GOBLET.

TWISTED CANE STEM

Preheat three short lengths of coloured rod canes by placing them side by side on a metal plate in the annealer. Gather a large bit of clear glass and marver it as if you were making a handle. Flash the bit over in the glory hole and then take it to the annealer, put the side of the bit on to the canes and hold the bit still for a few seconds to allow the canes to fuse to the side. You will now have a bit that is semicircular in section, with the canes on the flat side. Ask your assistant to gather another bit of glass, marver it lightly and then lay it on to the flat side of the original bit and cut the new glass. This will have trapped the canes in the centre. Warm the stem bit in the glory hole so that the join can no longer be seen. The stem bit can now be drawn into a long cane. Ask your assistant to hold the end of the bit with tweezers and then stretch the bit as you turn the iron in one direction to twist the canes. You will probably be able to pull enough to make three or four stems. Allow the cane to cool and then cut it to the required length with a file. Place the stems back in the annealer to warm them up. Blow up a wine glass bowl and then ask your assistant to pick up one of the already made stems from the annealer on a punty. He should now warm the end of the stem in the glory hole and bring it to you as if it were a punty. Grasp the iron with the jacks and stick the end of the stem to the bowl. Jack down where the punty and stem are joined and give the iron a sharp tap. The bit iron will come free. Warm the whole glass at the glory hole and finish shaping the stem. Add a foot and complete the glass in the usual way.

LATTICINO STEM

A Latticino style stem can be made by picking coloured canes up out of an optic mould on to a hot stem bit. The canes are heated on to the sides of the stem bit and then cast on to the wine-glass bowl. Another, simpler method is to pick up the impression from the optic mould on to a clear stem bit and then roll the clear glass in coloured powdered glass. The powder will settle into the valleys of the ridged stem bit. Warm the bit thoroughly at the glory hole and then cast it on to the base of the wine glass. You must remember to roll the glass in one direction only as you draw out the stem so that the twist is even down the length of the stem.

AIR TWIST STEM

Air twist stem glasses always impress. There is quite a knack to making these and they will require a lot of practice. Begin by gathering a first, small gather on a blowing iron. Marver the gather to a cylinder and then put four creases into the glass. Make the creases with the blades of the jacks. Squeeze the glass with the jacks on either side of the gather, making two creases. Turn the iron through 90 degrees and squeeze with the jacks again, making four creases. The indentations need to come two-thirds up the clear gather. After you have made the creases, thumb in a small bubble. You now need to gather again. With practice, as you gather on this shape, you will trap four bubbles where the creases are. Take the new gather to the bench and, working quickly, block as much of the hot, fresh glass to the end of the hard, first gather as possible. Try not to squeeze too hard because you will lose the bubbles. Take the diamond shears and cut off all of the surplus hot glass that you have blocked to the end. Blow down the iron until the bubble is the size needed for the wine glass. Reheat the glass at the glory hole and then cut down the neck. Draw out the stem, remembering to turn the glass in one direction only to keep the twist even. You may find that there is still a large amount of waste glass on the stem and so shear away any surplus with the diamond shears. Be careful not to squeeze out the air twists by overworking the stem. The air twist goblet that is illustrated was made by Anthony Wassell, an absolute master of this difficult technique.

The Foot

Step three is adding the foot. While your assistant is gathering a 'foot bit', flash the wine glass all over in the glory hole. The size of the foot bit and the delivery method are the same as for the stem. Stop the bit iron turning with your shears and let the hot glass fall on to the end of the stem; cut it free and then quickly return the blowing iron to the horizontal position across the arms of the bench. Pick up the foot tool from the wet tool bucket. Open the hinge of the tool and gently but quickly tap the hot glass back to the centre and push it so that you can feel the harder glass of the stem hindering you from pushing any further. The hot glass should now be in a round, fluffy, cushion shape. Close the hinge and apply a small amount of pressure with your thumb, while increasing the speed at which you turn the pipe. Gradually increase the force with which you squeeze and the speed of your roll and you will see the hot glass form into a flat disc. You should be able to complete the process in about two full-length rolls of the bench. As soon as the foot has spun out, return the foot tool to the water. Flash the whole glass over in the glory hole while your assistant prepares a punty.

Anthony Wassell: AIR TWIST COLLECTION.

Even the factories that profess to make their wine glasses by hand will stop at this point and put the glass into the annealer. When the glass is cold, they then cut the top off the bubble and polish the edge back to make the rim of the glass. The true hand-finishing process should take place on the punty iron.

BLOWN FEET

The blown foot, if made correctly, makes almost any piece of stemware look like high quality. The thinness of a blown foot adds an extra level of delicacy that a spun foot cannot do. To make a blown foot, ask your assistant to blow a small bubble of about two-thirds of the final diameter required and neck it down neatly. There are two main ways in which the foot is attached to the stem. The first and the simpler is to ask your assistant to heat up the tip of the bubble that he has just blown for you and then present it to you as if it were a punty. Grasp

the iron with your jacks and stick the bubble to the stem, roll the two irons together, jacking down on the neck of the bubble. The bubble is then knocked off the blowing iron, leaving it attached to the stem. Take the object (such as a wine glass) to the glory hole, heat the foot as if it were the rim of any ordinary vessel and open it to the shape required.

The second way of attaching the bubble to the stem is to ask your assistant to heat the whole bubble and present it as if it were a regular, solid, foot bit. Snip the bubble on to the stem in the normal spun foot method. Heat the tip of the foot bubble in the glory hole and, when you return to the bench, pull a slight point at the base of the foot by using the tweezers. Make a mark with the jacks about 12mm (½in) from the tip of the point that you have just made and allow it to cool. Gently file around the jacked mark and then tap the point of the bubble to knock the end off. Reheat the bubble at the glory hole and shape the foot as required.

Most blown feet are finished with a folded rim to strengthen the edge. To keep the foot looking attractive and delicate the rim is best folded inside. To do this you need to heat the rim to a slighter higher temperature than usual and then flatten the rim and the next 12mm (½in) with the bow of the jacks. Reheat the bubble and then drive open the foot as you gently push the rim inwards. Keep opening the foot, without returning to the glory hole, until the rim sticks back on to the side of the bubble. Make sure that it is firmly stuck around the entire circumference; if there is any point that is not fully attached it will try to separate off when you next reheat. You can now flare the foot to the required shape, which is generally more domed than a spun foot.

Hand Finishing

Stage four is the hand finishing and is exactly the same as for the tumbler. Greater care has to be taken when you are reheating the glass at the glory hole. If you do not heat it up enough, the stem and the foot will crack; too much heat, and the stem and the foot will wobble and bend out of control. Try to finish the glass in no more than three reheatings and be sure at each that you fully flash the wine glass in the glory hole. When you put the glass into the annealer you should place it on its rim to avoid the foot from bending during the cooling cycle. Make yourself a 'goblet fork' out of an old piece of wood for putting wine glasses into the annealer. You will need a piece of wood about 90cm (3ft) long that is narrow enough to hold in one hand but wide enough for you to cut a notch out of the other end, about 25mm (1in) wide, by 75mm (3in) deep. With this tool you can pick up a wine glass which is upside down from below the foot and reach to the back of your annealer without getting burned.

Handles

Having attempted to make a wine glass you are now aware of how necessary it is to have a good assistant working with you; even if he is highly skilled you need to build up a relationship between yourself and him. The consistency in having the same foot bit brought to you over and over again will improve your ability. Putting handles on to jugs, pitchers and tankards requires understanding between the maker and the assistant.

To make handles you will need a copper pipe, a pair of tweezers and your diamond shears. You need them all in the tool bay, available at a moment's notice. With a jug or tankard on the punty and almost finished, ask your assistant to bring you a handle. He needs to gather about as much glass for the average pitcher handle as he would for a foot bit. The gather is taken to the marver and rolled on the plate. With the minimum of contact with the marver, the glass needs to be rolled out to a cylinder. The gather is then taken to the gaffer. At the gaffer's request, the assistant moves the iron from the horizontal to the vertical, with the glass pointing downwards. The gaffer should hold the iron with the diamond shears and place the handle at the required position on the vessel. Most handles become thinner as they move upwards, so you are placing the handle gather at the base of the finished handle. Stretch the handle upwards slightly, release the iron and cut through the handle at a warm place in the bit about a quarter of the way towards the blown vessel. It is important to cut at a point that is hot. Quickly turn the punty iron through 180 degrees so that the handle is pointing to the floor. Be careful not to let the handle fall to the sides of the blown piece. Put the shears down and quickly pick up the copper pipe, turn the punty iron through a further 180 degrees, so the handle passes you on the way up, slide the copper pipe under the handle as it falls towards the glass and carry the tip of the handle with the copper pipe to where you wish to attach it; by using the copper pipe, push the tip of the handle into the body of the vessel, ensuring the remainder of the handle does not collapse and stick to the glass in the wrong place. Take the whole piece to the glory hole and give it a flash over. Finally, take the glass back to the bench and shape the handle to the required form.

There are many things that may go wrong when making handles. The most common problem is an over-marvered bit. If the handle is too stiff when you attach it to the body of your object, grasp the tip of the bit with the tweezers instead of the copper pipe and push it into the body of the object while it is still pointing downwards. After it has been flashed over, use the copper pipe to shape the handle. The second most common problem is that the bit is too hot when it reaches you. In this case cut the base as normal but keep the handle pointing upwards for a second or two. The bit will fall back on to itself. By using your judgement, turn the punty through 180 degrees and the handle will drop to the length that you need and be at the required temperature as it gets to that length. Use the copper pipe as explained earlier to place and shape the handle. If you let the handle get too cold, quickly pick up the tweezers to finish it.

As you can see, there are many variables to be held in mind when you are making handles and you need to be completely focused so that you can change your routine at a moment's notice. Making handles is a real test of skill, ability and the understanding between the maker and the assistant.

E+M Glass: DOODLE PITCHER.

OPPOSITE PAGE:
TOP: **Placing the handle bit.**

BOTTOM: **Stretching the handle.**

THIS PAGE:
ABOVE: **Catching the handle with the copper pipe.**

ABOVE RIGHT: **Attaching the top of the handle.**

RIGHT: **Shaping the handle.**

Margaret Burke: MARINE LIFE.

CHAPTER 6

TROUBLESHOOTING

Be Prepared

As you read this book and work through the different techniques, some things will go wrong. William Morris, one of the greatest glassmakers of our time, once told me that from the second that you gather glass from the furnace you begin correcting your mistakes. Mistakes do happen and the wise glassmaker uses these to broaden his knowledge of the way glass behaves. No two gathers of glass will act in exactly the same way, and so, over time, you need to develop a mental encyclopaedia of solutions to problems to achieve regular and consistent results. We all learn by making mistakes and getting things wrong – try not to be too hard on yourself or your assistants while you are learning new things. Every technique will need to be done with the glass too hot and too cold before the correct temperature is learned. Similarly, everything will need to be done too quickly and too slowly for you to discover the correct pace that is needed. Most experienced glassmakers from time to time will find that a particular problem will creep into their glass-making and not go away; at these times you need to step back and analyse what you are doing in order to assess what is going wrong. I shall outline some common problems and their cures here, but this will be by no means a complete list and never could be. Practice is generally the best solution, but it is to be hoped that these tips will help to reduce the pain.

Off-Centre Bubble Problems

Check to see whether your blowpipe is straight: you can do this by rolling it up and down your bench. If it is bent you will see the tip move up and down as you roll. If you use a bent pipe it will be difficult to centre the freshly gathered glass on the iron, and if the iron is not at the centre of the glass as you blow down the pipe the bubble will be off-centre. Your pipe manufacturer will be able to straighten out bent blowing irons for you, but if your pipes regularly bend out of shape you will need to learn to be more gentle with them. Try not to heat the iron up too much when you are heating the glass at the glory hole; when the iron is hot it may easily be knocked out of shape.

If your first gather is uneven and you have to work hard to smooth it out, the bubble will almost certainly go off-centre. If you have had to work hard to tidy up a gather, try reheating it in the glory hole to even out the temperatures *before* you thumb in the bubble. If uneven gathers are a regular problem you will need to work on your gathering technique. Most gathering problems stem from erratic pipe turning, you will need to turn the pipe at a constant and even speed all the time. When you are gathering glass, when you are walking around your studio, when you are working on the glass with various tools, you always need to turn the pipe at a constant, even speed so that the glass does not drop off-centre. If your first gather is off-centre and you put a bubble into it, any second and third gathers will only compound and exacerbate the problem rather than hide or cure it.

Another common way of putting the bubble off-centre is the action of thumbing the bubble. It is likely that at some point, while you are still mastering the technique, the pipe will cease to roll for a fraction of a second; at this point the glass will droop towards the floor and the bubble will come into the glass off-centre. If the glass does so droop, quickly turn it over so that the lowest point of the glass is now the highest and wait for it to fall back on centre. If you push the glass back on centre with newspaper or some tool, you will create a cold spot on one side that will itself cause the bubble to blow off-centre. The glass is softer and more malleable when it is hot, so the air will always move to the warmest part of the glass.

Quite often the problem has more than one cause and so the solution is likely to require a combination of techniques. It is also much easier for someone else to see what you are doing wrong than it is to see it yourself. If there is experienced help around ask for advice, remember that everybody has suffered from these problems at some time in the past.

Cracking-Off Problems

Another common problem for inexperienced glassmakers is an inability to remove blown glass from the blowpipe. There are three main reasons for this: the shape of the glass at the cut down, the thickness or, more correctly, the weight distribution of the glass, and the temperature of the glass.

The shape of the glass at the point where the cut down is made is vitally important. At the cut down point, lean the jacks into the blown glass to create a small 'S' shape at the neck. This action is sometimes known as 'laying off' or 'necking in'. If the glass is cold, making it difficult to cut down and lay off, flash the glass over at the glory hole before you try to remove it from the blowing iron. Any imbalance of temperature may also create problems in removing the glass.

The second most common reason for such difficulties is the thickness of the glass. It is perfectly possible to make very thick pieces of glass; it is the thickness of the rim relative to the rest of the object that is crucial. The glass needs to be blown in such a way that the rim is the thinnest part, with the walls gradually becoming thicker as you get to the thickest point at the base. To check that your bubbles are blown correctly you will need to split one open and examine the walls: if the base is too thin, you can remedy this by chilling the bottom of the glass with a newspaper pad while your assistant blows down the pipe for you at the bench. This action will inflate the shoulders of the glass while leaving the base as it is. But if you have no assistant you can put a paper pad on the floor and blow against that yourself. A useful adjunct to have is a rubber tube that can be attached over the pipe mouthpiece at one end while you blow down the other end of the tubing; in this way you can paper the bottom of the glass and blow it yourself from a seated position at the bench. Another solution is to make the shape of the glass longer before you put any air into it; the bubble will always try to inflate into a sphere and so by lengthening the glass before you put any air into it you are creating a thicker base.

The third reason why glass will not become detached from the blowing iron relates to the temperature. If the glass is too hot, so that it is still moving, it will be difficult to break. Sometimes, when the glass is too hot, the outside of the glass breaks but the inside is still attached. You and your assistant end by pulling at your irons while a few stringy pieces of hot glass prevent you from separating, rather like two pieces of pizza being held together by the cheese topping. The problem here is the difference in temperature between the inside and the outside of the glass; you need the inside of the glass to cool down without the outside getting too cold; here the remedy is simple but time-consuming. You need a series of short flashes at the glory hole; the short flash prevents the heat from penetrating too deeply into the wall of the glass. By this method the inside of the glass cools down slowly as you gently heat up the outside. After a few flashes the inside and the outside will have evened out enough in temperature for it to be possible to remove the glass from the blowing iron. Many thick pieces of glass that are placed straight into the annealer without this series of flashes to even out the temperatures will crack within a few days after they have cooled down. This quick flashing procedure on thick glass may, in many ways, be viewed as the start of the annealing process.

Temperature is also responsible for problems for another reason. Quite often the glass is left to get too cold before you try to separate it. In this instance everyone's immediate reaction is to saw and file away at the cut down and then to give the iron a thump, which generally results in the breaking of the object you are blowing into many pieces or of knocking a few chips out of the rim. Sometimes after the thump the glass will separate perfectly well, only to explode as you take it to the glory hole. When the procedure for removing the glass works successfully, the glass will break at the cut-down point because of thermal shock, not because of how much you saw or file the mark. The cut-down and file marks are guidelines for the direction in which the glass will crack, in much the same way that a scratch line made with a cutter on flat glass is to guide the crack and not to cut it. To remove the glass successfully some heat is needed in the glass itself and then the cut down is chilled with the jacks, a file or some water. Tap the blowing iron sharply with the bow of the jacks or a wooden block as soon as possible after the glass has chilled and the glass will separate at the cut-down point. Excessive sawing and filing only create a larger cold spot and so, in turn, a larger number of places for the glass to break at. If you find that you are having difficulty in separating the glass, try not to saw and file more because they will only make the problem worse instead of better. As usual, it is generally a combination of several factors that will be causing your problem and so a combination of solutions will be needed to alleviate the situation.

Gathering Problems

Many people experience misshapen and uneven gathers. The reason is that the pipe has been unevenly or insufficiently turned in the glass during the gathering process. This happens because the worker who is gathering is in a hurry. A bit gatherer may be rushing to fetch a stem or foot bit and, in his eagerness to be efficient, will cause himself more problems. The main reason for hurrying when gathering is to escape the heat of the furnace, but there are a few things that can be done to make gathering less intimidating: you could wear an old sock with the toes removed over your left arm as you gather, as described earlier; moving where you stand may well make the action of gathering less painful, as may also opening the door of the furnace only as much as you need to in order to get the gathered glass out; ask an assistant to move the door for you as you gather and ask him to close the opening down as you gather and then open it up to allow you to get away with the glass. There is no merit in being burned or scorched by the furnace; protect yourself from the heat and ask for help from your assistant.

Having got a good, even gather and taken it back to the bench, you find that it has spun out into a flat disc or will be well on its way to doing so. You try to paper or block it to shape and end by creasing and folding the glass, trapping air and ash as you go, and there will be visible hot and cold spots all over the surface of the gather. This will be a familiar scenario to most glassmakers at some time in their careers. Quite simply, the glass is being moved too fast; slow down the speed at which you are turning the iron or turn the temperature of the glass down at the furnace so that gravity does not take control. It is worth noting, that the more glass you gather, the slower the rate at which you need to turn the iron. Why you have multiple gathers on a blowing iron it is always a good idea to get your assistant to help in rolling the iron up and down the bench, but make sure that he does not turn the iron too quickly nor too slowly.

If you are finding it difficult to collect very much glass when you are gathering, first try turning the temperature of the furnace down. If this does not improve things, try guarding your left arm with an old sock, and, if this still does not improve things, you need to examine your action when you gather. Place the tip of the iron into the glass to about 2.5cm (1in) and make at least one complete revolution in the glass. Keep turning, but move the tip of the iron across the surface of the glass towards the back of the furnace. Next, as you lift the iron from the glass, increase the speed at which you turn the iron. This speeding up will collect much more glass, and then, as you leave the glass, a thin strand of glass will remain and break in the heat of the furnace. In this way you can keep the glass on the iron rather than watch it all fall back into the furnace whence it came.

Punty Problems

There are many problems to overcome when your glass is on the punty iron. The first that you will encounter will almost certainly be that the glass will fall off the iron before you are finished; the prime explanation for this will be that the punty join has become too cold. The punty must be kept warm at all times; when you are warming up the rim of a glass at the glory hole you must remember to flash the whole glass over, including the punty, at regular intervals. As you come out of the glory hole, there should be a tiny degree of movement in the punty joint; if the punty becomes too hot at any point, it may be almost impossible to take the finished glass from the iron, as having too hot a punty will weld the joint to the base of the glass just as if it were a stem or a foot of a wine glass.

It is the case that many pieces of glass end up as plant pots because as the punty is being removed from the finished object a hole appears in the bottom of the glass. The most common reason for this is that the bottom of the glass was blown thinner than the rest of the object; if it was difficult to get the glass from the blowing iron to the punty, you will have almost certainly blown the bottom too thin. Another reason for the appearance of holes in the bottom of finished glassware is the punty's being too large for the object. In this case try using a narrower iron or a different style of punty; there are many different types of punty joint developed to suit various situations and needs (*see* Chapter 4 on punty making and learn new styles to try out). Holes may also be caused by the glass and the punty becoming too cold; this is a common problem on very long objects. The only solution is to keep the bottom of the glass warmer; if the glass is so long that it will not fit into the glory hole, use a blow torch on its base when you are back at your bench.

CHAPTER 7

USING COLOUR

Now that you have whet your appetite on basic glass blowing, it is time to study some more advanced techniques. The use of colour is one of the defining qualities of studio glass. The creative use of concentrated coloured rods and powders is one of the main ways in which glass artists can express themselves; innovative methods for joining two or more pieces of glass together further release imaginative abilities. You should use these techniques as starting points to develop your own methods and personal style as a glass artist, but it is of the utmost importance that the techniques do not dictate to you what you make, instead they need to be an aid to your creativity, you need to design the object you wish to make and have as clear a vision as possible of what you are trying to create. The next step is to decide which are the most appropriate skills to use.

THIS PAGE:
E+M Glass:
SQUASH RANGE.

OPPOSITE PAGE:
Jane Charles:
RIPPLE-RIMMED VASE.

Elementary Colour Methods

In days gone by, glass was coloured by adding a few grams of chemicals to the furnace as you were melting glass. Compounds of cobalt would produce blue, those of manganese would produce purple and those of iron would produce green, for example. Streaks of colour would run through the glass at random intervals. If the chemicals were added to the batch before melting a more even colour tint would be produced. In these ways the entire body of the glass would be stained one colour. If you required a second colour, a second furnace was needed and a third colour meant that a third furnace was imperative, and so on. The cost implications for the small glass producer and for the glass artist were crippling. Thankfully, there are now a number of small factories producing a large 'palette' of concentrated coloured glasses which can be added to clear glass during the blowing process. These producers offer their colours in a number of forms; the standard one is a solid bar weighing about 0.5kg (1lb). Grinding these bars yields grits and rocks that may be applied to the glass in numerous ways. Most makers of coloured glasses offer a range of grits and rocks which range from fine, floury grades, through sugary grades, to small chips and larger rocks. The grinding process adds considerably to the cost of the colour, but I would still recommend that you buy it already ground rather than do it yourself; it can be done in your own studio but it is a very wasteful process and will work out cheaper in the long run to buy it in the form in which you want to use it. In addition to the form the coloured glass takes, it may also be bought as either opaque or transparent colour. These concentrated coloured bars are often referred to as Kugler, after Klaus Kugler who set up and ran the factory that was the main producer of coloured glass for the studio glass market, but there are many other producers of concentrated colour world-wide. Kugler colours are now manufactured by Friedrich Farbglashütte who have world-wide distribution partners. Gaffer Glass was formed in 1993 in New Zealand and has quickly grown to be a major supplier of concentrated colour. They are reknowned for a very high quality product. Other companies such as Zimmerman, Reichenbach, and Ornella also supply quality colours. All of these companies have distribution agents throughout the world. C & R Loo, Hot Glass Color & Supply, Kugler Colors, Olympic Color and Gaffer all have good websites and a few minutes on the Internet should unveil the nearest supplier to you.

ABOVE: **Coloured glass Kugler rods.**

ABOVE RIGHT: **Coloured glass grains.**

RIGHT: **Coloured glass powder.**

Using these types of colour is a slow process in comparison with blowing clear glass and so you must be sure that the addition of colour to the piece also adds worth to the final object; this use of the word does not relate just to the price of the final object, it also refers to the aesthetics of the finished piece. These coloured glasses are highly concentrated, they are made to be used with clear glass. The basic principle is to make a thin skin of colour on either the inner or the outer surface of the clear glass, giving the illusion of the colour going right through the object; the highly concentrated colour is often not apparent until it has been thinly stretched over the clear.

Rod Colour

The primary way to add colour to a blown vessel would be to use the solid bars to put a layer of colour on to the inside of the object. Choose a coloured bar and cut a piece about 2.5cm (1in) long and put it into a small kiln, set at around 550°C (1,020°F), to preheat. The easiest way to cut coloured rods is to use a flat-bed electric tile saw; ceramic tile saws have a small, circular, diamond-impregnated blade cooled by water. Cut the rods slowly, letting the blade do the cutting. Do make sure that water is being picked up by the blade as it rotates; if the wheel is dry it will heat up the glass and make it sticky. If both the blade and the glass get hot, the glass will strip the diamonds from the blade and ruin it. Try not to push too hard since excessive force may cause the bar to crack and split in the wrong place. If you do not have access to a tile saw, a chisel may be used; use the type of chisel that a bricklayer would use, as opposed to a woodworker. When you are cutting with a chisel, tap lightly on all sides of the bar at the point where you want it to cut; tap round the bar again, hitting slightly harder; keep tapping and increasing the strength of the taps. With practice, you will be able to cut quite accurately.

If you need to cut small pieces and do not have a tile saw, cut a large piece and warm it up slowly in the kiln, raise the temperature of the colour by picking it up on a bit iron and putting it into the glory hole; when it is hot you can then use your diamond shears to cut the required amount of colour. Put the extra piece of colour back into the kiln for later. If you do not have a small kiln available for heating up colour there are a number of other things that you can try: many glassmakers put their colour into the annealer to preheat; if you do this, you will have to be careful when you come to pick up the colour to use it. By using the annealer, which will be set between 450 and 480°C (about 870°F), the colour will not be

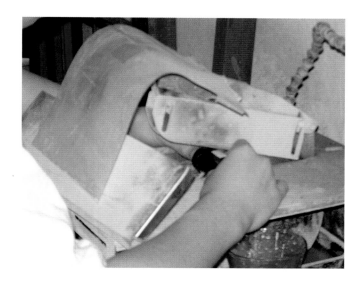

Cutting the rods on a tile saw.

Cutting the rods with a chisel.

quite hot enough and may crack. It may crack internally without the outside showing any signs of damage, this results in bubbles in the colour, known as blisters. As an alternative to the annealer for preheating, the coloured glass may be placed on a piece of angle iron close to the mouth of the furnace or the glory hole; start with the colour about 30cm (12in) away from the heat and gradually move it closer and closer over a period of 10 to 15min. If you move it towards the heat too quickly, the colour will crack, so be careful, but if you move it too close, it may stick to the angle iron. With practice, you will find places where you can put the colour that are neither too hot nor too cold. The best environment for warming up colour is one that can be controlled and reproduced easily, which is why I prefer to use a small kiln.

Once the colour is warmed through it can be attached to the nose of the blowing iron, the colour then becoming the first gather of glass. Subsequent gathers are made in clear glass from the furnace. As the glass is inflated the colour becomes a thin skin on the inside of the object; the inside layer of colour may be seen through the outside clear glass, giving the object the appearance of being coloured through its entire body.

To attach the preheated coloured rod to the blowing iron you will need to use one of the following methods. If you are preheating the colour in a top-loading kiln, warm the tip of your blowing iron to slightly hotter than the normal cherry red; lift the lid on the kiln with your left hand and, with your right holding the blowing iron, firmly press the nose of the iron on to the colour for a few seconds. Remove the iron, with the colour fixed to it, from the kiln and invert the iron so that the colour is directed upwards. Gravity is now keeping the colour on the end of the pipe. Close the lid of the kiln and take the blowpipe to the glory hole to heat the colour thoroughly. With practice, you will be able to pick up the colour and reach the glory hole quickly enough so that the colour is still above 450°C. If you are fast enough, you can put the iron and colour straight into the mouth of the glory hole. However, if you are slow, the temperature will have dropped below 450°C and the glass may crack. In this situation put the iron on to the glory-hole yoke with the colour about 10cm (4in) from the heat. Over a period of 30sec or so, gradually move the colour into the heat; if it is a small piece you can move into the heat faster, but if it is large you may need to take longer.

If you are using your annealer to warm the colour you will need to put an extra step into the routine. Pushing into a piece of colour with a blowpipe for a few seconds in the annealer may cause damage to already finished objects by your leaving the door open for too long. The quickest way of getting in and out of the annealer is to get a tiny piece of clear glass from the furnace on the end of a punty iron and make a very hot punty; go to the annealer, open the door very slightly and stick the punty to the required coloured bar. It is a good idea to place the colour as high up in the annealer as you can, the top is almost always hotter than the bottom. Remove the punty with the colour coupled to it and close the door quickly, move to the glory hole and hold the colour about 10cm (4in) from the heat. Gradually move the colour inside the heat and warm it completely through. When the colour is moving as freely as if it had been gathered from the furnace, attach it to a blowing iron in the same manner as you would a stem bit on a wine glass; give the punty iron with the colour on it to your assistant and ask him to approach you from the right-hand side; place the mouthpiece of the blowing iron you wish to use on the top of your foot. Ask your assistant to raise both hands above his head and allow the coloured glass to fall from the iron; grab the tip of the iron with your diamond shears and guide the coloured glass on to the tip of the blowing iron. For colour that you have warmed up in front of the furnace or glory hole, you may use either method, depending upon how hot the colour is. Be wary of getting the colour too hot in using this method because it may stick to the angle iron that it is resting on. If the angle iron gets too hot at any point it may begin to scale and flake, then these little pieces of metal may stick to the colour and ruin the finished object. It will be difficult to see these metal fragments until the next day when the glass has cooled down. The repeated use of colour on the nose of the blowing iron will make tiny traces of colour creep up the inside the blowpipe, then at some point this colour will come back down the iron and cause a dirty smear on the inside of your glass. To avoid this you can protect the iron by putting a small layer of clear glass on to the iron before you add the colour, this ensures that there is only clear glass going up the pipe. The colour is difficult to control with clear behind it and so I would not recommend that you begin using colour in this way. Let your ability grow and your confidence increase before you attempt this.

The colour should be shaped as if it were a first gather from the furnace. Coloured glass is prone to ash marks and so I would also recommend the use of either the bow of the jacks or a colour paddle to shape the glass. A colour paddle is a metal blade about 15cm (6in) long mounted on a handle; the idea of the paddle is to keep it only for this job so that it does not get dirty and risk soiling the glass. Then once the colour is shaped, thumb a bubble into the glass and watch carefully, do not let it inflate too far; if it becomes too thin, it will collapse as you gather more glass on top. Every colour has its own characteristics and will behave differently from any other; some will appear to warm quickly and others will feel as if they are taking forever to do so. Coloured glasses are referred to as either 'soft' or 'hard' colours; the terms refer to the amount of heat required to get the glass to move. You should make notes every time you try a new colour or a new

RIGHT: **Picking up the colour from a top-loading kiln.**

BELOW: **Shaping the heated up colour.**

BELOW RIGHT: **Shaping the clear glass gather on top of the colour.**

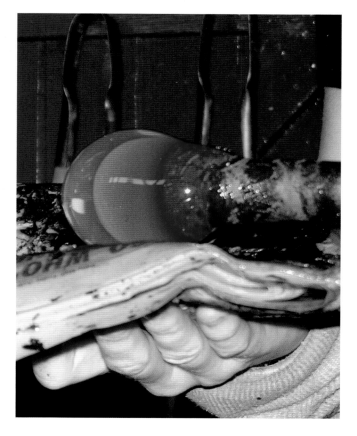

manufacturer of colours. You may find that you need to alter the temperature of your kiln to suit individual colours; you may find that a temperature 10 or 20°C cooler prevents soft colours from sticking to the floor of the kiln, while, at the same time, 10 or 20°C warmer and the hard colours will cease to crack at the glory hole. Your notes will help you to avoid putting soft colours in the kiln at a hard colour temperature and vice versa. If you use hard and soft colours on the same object you will generally find that the soft colour will inflate much easier than the hard one; this will cause the walls of the object to be thicker at the hard colour and thinner at the soft. But this is not necessarily a problem, however, you can use this phenomenon to your advantage. For example, if you put a hard colour on to the bottom of a piece it will be difficult to blow it too thin to make it possible to attach a punty.

Powdered Colour

Powdered coloured glass is used to put a layer of colour on to the outside of an object instead of the inside. Whereas rod colour gives an even wash of colour, powder may be patchy and textural, with the effect depending on the size of the grains used. Two main methods of applying powder are commonly used. First, coloured grains can be laid out on the marver and hot glass gathered from the furnace immediately rolled into it; this method has the advantage that more than one colour can be easily rolled on to the glass at the same time, but the major disadvantage is that the grains do tend to stick together and give uneven patches of colour. This may be used to great effect with some forethought. The second main way of applying powdered

Rolling on powdered colour from the marver.

Jane Charles:
CUT SEAFORM WITH
GLASS PEBBLES.

colour is to shake it on to hot glass through a loose sieve. The main advantage of this method is the even coating of colour that is given; the major disadvantage is the great dust hazard that is created; it is very unwise to sieve colour if you do not have a good extraction unit to remove airborne dust. It is wise to have a cabinet built with a yoke to rest the blowpipe with the hot glass on it; at the bottom of the cabinet there should be a bowl to catch the surplus powder as it is sieved, and at the top of the box there should be an extractor fan to take away all dust and harmful fumes. Care should also be taken when applying colour from the marver not to create a dust hazard.

Compatibility is a major problem when using colour; when you add colour to a piece of glass in this way you are, in effect, mixing two completely different glasses together – the coloured glass and the clear. You need to know what the coefficient of expansion of each glass is. The coefficient of expansion may be considered as a measure of how much each glass moves as it cools down: if one glass moves more than the other, stress will be created in the final object and it will almost certainly crack. It may not crack for weeks or months, but the stress is in the glass and so at some point it will need to be relieved. Most coloured glass manufacturers produce glass with an expansion around $95 \times 10^{-7}°K$. You should check with your batch or cullet supplier what the coefficient of expansion is of the clear glass. The important part of the value number is the first set of digits, often the rest of the expression is dropped and people talk in terms of 'an expansion of 98', for example. Try to use colour that differs by no more than ±2 of the expansion of the clear glass. Soda glasses need to be much nearer than lead or barium glasses to the expansion of the coloured glass; the softer glasses are generally more tolerant of shrinkage and expansion during annealing than are harder glasses.

Many artists, such as Siddy Langley, Jane Charles and Anthony Stern, use clear glass and colour with these techniques to stunning ends. By applying the many rods, powders and grains at different times and stages spectacular images can be built up.

Siddy Langley: BLOWN AND SANDCAST.

Advanced Colour Techniques

Sandblasting

Sandblasting is one of the most commonly used techniques in studio glass. This is a process that is performed when the glass is cold, it removes large areas of colour to reveal clear glass or another coloured layer underneath. A sandblaster is a machine that fires a fine jet of sand or some other abrasive at a surface with a high-pressure jet, pushed by air from a compressor, at strengths between 1.4 and 9.8kg/sq cm (20 and 140lb/sq in); the higher the pressure the faster the colour is worn away. The high pressure also gives a coarse grain effect as opposed to a smooth, low-pressure finish.

The sandblaster itself generally comprises a metal cabinet. There will be two arm holes in the front with a pair of heavy-gauge rubber gloves attached to them. Above the holes there is a window so that you can see into the unit. There will be a door, either at the front or the side, to allow the glass to be placed inside the cabinet. At the bottom is a hopper to collect the grit after it has bounced off the glass; this allows a relatively small amount of abrasive to be continuously recycled as the machine is used. There is a large amount of dust created by sandblasting so a good extractor unit needs to be fitted (without one you will be unable to see what you are doing after only a few seconds). The air compressor will need to have a device attached to dry the air; drying units can be fitted near to the compressor and moisture traps attached at the sandblaster itself; a tiny amount of moisture in the forced air will make the abrasive stick together in large lumps and clog up the system.

Several methods are used to protect the areas of glass that you do not wish to erode. The most common is to cover the surface of the glass completely with an adhesive-backed plastic and then, with a sharp craft knife, cut away plastic to reveal the areas that you wish to sandblast. Another method of masking the glass before sandblasting is to paint the surface direct with wood glue; you can paint with a brush or pipe it

on by squeezing a plastic bottle and extruding the glue over the surface of the glass. Allow the glue to dry to a rubbery consistency, sandblast the glass and then remove the glue by placing the object into warm water. The glue will soften and float away from the surface. A number of companies produce sandblasting stencils; a huge amount of fine detail can be achieved by using stencils. You will need to reduce the required image down to just black and white; a transfer is then made by using photographic techniques; these you then attach to the glass. Such transfers are very delicate and need to be used under the lightest air pressures. This method is useful if you have a number of identical objects to make; the photographic methods mean that an unlimited number of copy transfers can be produced.

Malcolm Sutcliffe's elephant bowl was engraved by using plastic as a mask. Much planning needs to go into making a piece like this; the positioning of the different layers of colour

Applying the glue sandblast resist.

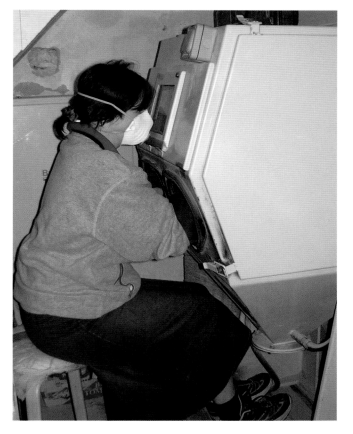

The sandblasting cabinet.

needs to be worked out in great detail before you start. Sutcliffe created the coloured surfaces in two layers: the inner one multicoloured and the outer one black. In its original form, the black would have completely covered the outside of the bowl. He would have then covered the bowl in sticky plastic and begun cutting out the elephant motifs (some artists cut the shapes out of the plastic before putting them on to glass); the bowl would have been put into the sandblasting cabinet and had the entire unmasked, top layer of black glass removed. After taking the bowl from the sandblaster the protective layer of plastic would be taken away and the stunning, finished piece revealed.

Margaret Burke uses wood glue to create her sandblasting masks. In contrast to the hard, precise edge that a plastic mask gives, glue masks are much more flowing and free in nature. She takes a plate with a single layer of colour on it; the positioning is worked out direct on the plate by using a waterproof black marker pen. When she is happy with the layout, glue is painted on to the surface. This is applied very thickly and is allowed to dry for some hours before being sandblasted. As with Malcolm Sutcliffe's bowl, the entire unprotected surface is again removed, but this time it reveals a layer of clear glass. The glue mask is less consistent in thickness than the plastic film and so from time to time the sandblaster will erode parts that have been masked. This may be avoided by painting numerous layers on top of each other or it is possible to let the mask be eroded, creating a more organic feel.

As your skill with the sandblaster improves you will find that you can introduce a degree of shading into your images. By lightly sandblasting an unmasked area, and not going completely through the colour, the density of the coloured glass will lighten. This has been used to great effect in this bowl (*opposite page*) by Margaret Burke.

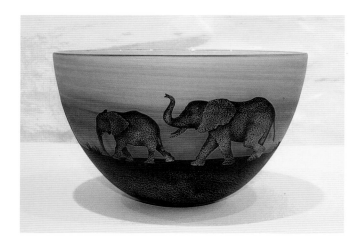

ABOVE: **Malcolm Sutcliffe:** ELEPHANT BOWL.

BELOW: **Margaret Burke:** MULTICOLOURED FISH.

BELOW RIGHT: **Margaret Burke:** AQUA FACE.

Margaret Burke: HAPPY FISH.

E+M Glass: CREATURES RANGE.

Incalmo

This is a wonderful technique for creating horizontal bands of colour. You will need a very good assistant or a top-loading kiln and a couple of pairs of measuring callipers. Begin by warming up two pieces of solid rod colour. Pick up the colour that you wish to be at the bottom of the finished piece; if you used a punty or bit iron to pick up the colour, transfer it to a blowing iron when it is hot. Get a small amount of air into the colour and then gather clear glass over the top. Blow up a small bubble, keeping the sides and rim quite thick. Attach the bubble to a punty iron, open it out into a small cup and accurately measure the diameter of the rim. You can now either ask your assistant to keep this bubble warm for 10min or so while you make the next piece, or you can place the cup into the top-loading kiln. If you place the cup rim downwards in the kiln, your assistant will need to pick it up for you later with a new punty. Alternatively, you can place the cup in the kiln in a ceramic ring, with the rim pointing upwards, similar to the setting up of a graal embryo (*see* page 123).

Warm up the second piece of colour, get some air into it and then gather some clear glass on top. Shape this gather to resemble a long bullet and then cut down a marble-sized ball at the end with the jacks. Gently blow the colour up until it reaches the marble. Slightly chill the sides of the bubble away from the marble and then heat the marble and just beyond it in the glory hole; be careful not to overheat. Go back to the bench and gently stretch the tip of the bubble 2 or 3cm (1in) by pushing the marble away from you with the jacks. Now cut down on the bubble where the marble used to be, making a little stem shape at the end of the bubble, but be sure not to cut down too far and seal the bubble. Let the bubble cool a little and then use your wet file on the new cut-down point. Give the stem shape a gentle tap and the end will fall off. You should now have a bubble with a hole at the end. Take the bubble to the glory hole and heat it up; back at the bench open up the bubble to the same size as that of the cup that you prepared earlier. If the cup is sitting in a ring in the top-loading kiln, rim upwards, open up the lid and carefully place your opened bubble on to the rim of the cup; allow a second or two for them to fuse together and then take them quickly to the glory hole to warm up. If the cup is rim-down in the kiln, ask your assistant to pick it up on a punty iron and warm it up in the glory hole. Next, your assistant should approach the bench with the cup as if it were a punty. Grasp the assistant's iron with the diamond shears and allow the cup to fall slightly. Now release your grip and the assistant should turn the iron through 180 degrees so that the cup is pointing slightly upwards. Grab the iron again; as the cup slowly falls back to the horizontal, push the two rims together to form one bubble then give the assistant's iron a sharp tap and it will become detached.

No matter how you joined the glasses together they need heating thoroughly at this point; any ridges from the join need to be completely melted out before blowing up the glass to its final shape. You can repeat the hollowing out process on this new bubble and join a second cup on to the bottom again if you wish. You can repeat this as many times as you wish, building up band after band of colour. One of the best exponents of this technique is Stuart Hearn. His powerful bowl (*see* page 122) has been made by using incalmo; the precision of his technique has allowed him to use simple areas of colour and simple lines to dramatic effect.

Incalmo requires a high degree of team work.

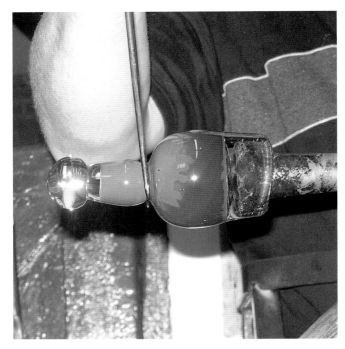

ABOVE LEFT: **The base cup.**

ABOVE RIGHT: **Opening the top cup.**

LEFT: **The top cup opened.**

Joining the top and
bottom cups together.

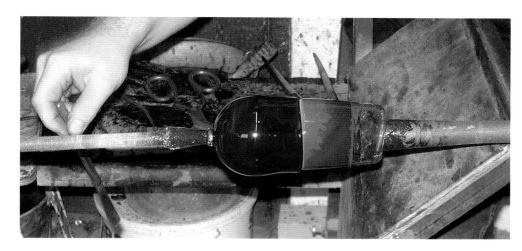

The two cups joined together.

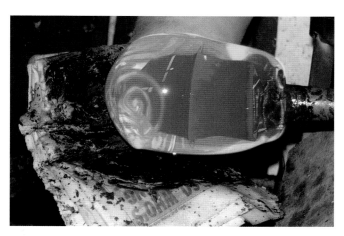

The two cups covered with a second gather of glass.

Finishing the piece.

Stuart Hearn:
BLUE STRATA BOWL.

Creating Horizontal Bands of Colour

In addition to the incalmo technique, there are a number of methods of creating horizontal bands of colour. One is to attach a piece of rod colour to the blowing iron and warm it up at the glory hole until it is molten. Take it back to the bench and shape it as if you were going to blow a bubble into it. But before you blow down the pipe, take the iron back to the glory hole and heat it through. At the bench take one of the blades of your jacks and push its point into the centre of the colour. Keep pushing and turning the iron until you can feel the solid iron preventing you from going any further. This needs to be done quickly, in less than a second in total. You should have a doughnut-shaped piece of coloured glass on the end of the blowing iron; blow firmly down the pipe and trap the air with your thumb. After a few seconds you should hear a loud pop as the air expands and bursts the thin layer of glass at the centre of the doughnut; if it does not pop straightaway, keep your thumb on the end of the iron and put the front of the pipe into the glory hole. After a few seconds the glass will burst. Warm the colour up in the glory hole, taking care not to get it too

hot; if it does get too hot, the hole in the centre will seal up and you will need to start again. When it is warm take the glass back to the bench and open up the rim to form a small cylinder. Meanwhile, your assistant will have been warming up another piece of coloured rod on a bit iron; get him to shape the colour to a cone, the widest part away from the iron. You will need to keep an eye on the temperature of the cylinder – neither too hot nor too cold. The assistant should now warm up the second piece of colour as much as he can and still keep it under control. He should approach the bench as if he was bringing you a punty. Grasp the bit iron with the diamond shears just behind the coloured glass; the bit will droop down. Release the pressure with the shears and your assistant should turn the iron through 180 degrees. Grasp the iron again and, as the glass falls through the horizontal, stick it to the end of the cylinder. Quickly cut through the colour, making sure that you do not leave any clear glass from the back of the bit in the piece that you have sheared on. While the bit is still hot, shape it with the bow of the jacks as if it were the first piece of colour and quickly thumb in some air. You will see a slight bulging in the second colour as the air expands; now you need to warm both pieces of colour up to the same temperature and get them to move as one. The colour may now be gathered over and made into your required shape.

As a matter of interest, it is important to make sure that the first colour is not too hot when you join the glasses together. You need the second piece to be the only one that is moving when you thumb the air in. The second colour must be cut, worked to shape and blown without any reheating because this will also warm the first colour and it will inflate instead of the second. This technique sounds complicated and difficult, but you should be able to master it fairly quickly; it is a very good way of placing areas of colour for sandblasting later.

Another good way of putting horizontal bands of colour is to place them on the outside of a clear post.

A clear post is a gather of glass that you block to shape and then put a bubble into; you should make it slightly cylindrical in shape. Ask your assistant to pick up a piece of rod colour and warm it in the glory hole. The bit needs to be marvered to a finger shape, slightly narrower at the end, and also needs to be heated in the glory hole so that it is warmer at the tip. The assistant should now bring it to you at the bench and present it to you hanging vertically, as if it were a handle. Grip the iron with the diamond shears, stick the tip of the colour on to the post and slowly roll the iron away from you. The slower you roll the thicker the trail of colour will be. Watch carefully for the colour as you roll, as you complete one full turn the colour should just overlap. Cut through the bit at this point and then warm the post and colour in the glory hole; this may be repeated as many times as you wish, building up layer after layer down the length of the post. When you have put as much colour on to the post as you require, heat the whole thoroughly, block it to an even, rounded shape and inflate it slightly. Allow it to cool a little and then you can gather on it and make the object that you have designed.

Threading

You can quickly add a line of colour to the glass by trailing. Make a post as before; meanwhile, ask your assistant to pick up a small piece of rod colour and warm it up. The colour should be marvered to a finger shape and then taken back to the glory hole and the tip reheated. The assistant should then bring the colour to the post, holding the iron vertically with the glass pointing downwards. Grip the iron with your diamond shears and touch the hot colour on to the post. Using a combination of stretching the colour with your right hand and rotating the post with

your left, you can lay down some interesting patterns. The most common use of this technique is to put a long spiral down the glass, rather like a barber's shop sign. To do this, have the post quite close to you on the bench and hold the iron in your finger tips. When your assistant approaches with the colour, stick it to the waste glass at the top of the post. Smoothly roll the iron down the bench by using your entire left arm. At the same time, gently push the colour away to the right and you should create a thin trail running right down the side of the post (*see* p.124).

There are a few refinements that you can make to the threaded post at this point. If you warmed the glass in the glory hole and then placed it into an optic mould, the threaded lines will form into little waves. If you used a knife or a spike on the threaded post, you can move the lines in different directions. These variations are known as combing and were very popular during the Art Nouveau era of Galle and Tiffany.

Graal

This is a wonderful technique that comes from Sweden. A coloured bubble, known as an embryo, has a sandblasted decoration applied to it; the bubble is reheated slowly over a number of hours and then picked up on a blowing iron. You may then either blow the bubble to the shape that you require or gather over the bubble and then blow the object. The hard, sandblasted edges will now soften and move with the rest of the molten glass creating a fluid, soft image.

The bubble may have a number of layers of colour to sandblast through and generally has an untouched, solid colour on the inside. The top layers of coloured glass can be applied as powders from the marver or be overlaid from solid bars. Overlaying is a difficult technique that results in the application of a layer of solid colour to the outside of a bubble. To overlay glass you will need the help of an assistant with a reasonable blowing ability. As you blow your bubble with solid rod colour inside it, ask your assistant to do the same thing at another bench. Fashion your bubble to a bullet shape and allow it to cool. Your assistant needs to make a bubble and then cut it in with the jacks. Your assistant should then reheat only the base of the bubble at the glory hole; the bubble is then brought to the gaffer as if it were a punty. The glassmaker then grasps the iron that the assistant is holding and sticks it to the bottom of the bullet-shaped gather. With a wet file, saw away at the cut down on the round bubble and give your assistant's blowing a sharp tap to detach it. Now return to the glory hole with the two bubbles on the one iron, give them both a long flash of heat and then concentrate on warming up

ABOVE LEFT: **Attaching the coloured bit.**

LEFT: **Rolling the bit over the post.**

BELOW LEFT: **Cutting through the trail with a knife.**

BELOW RIGHT: **The finished effect.**

the rim of the assistant's bubble. Open it out with the jacks as if it were a bowl. Return to the glory hole and heat the glass such that the assistant's bubble spins out into a small plate. With the wooden jacks push the glass plate backwards over the bullet-shaped bubble. This may take three or four reheats to do neatly, but make sure that you do not trap any air or crease the coloured plate as you fold it back.

The overlaid bubble is sandblasted in exactly the same way as any other glass object. Some glass artists engrave the embryo with a dentist's drill to get a very fine line quality. You could always combine both sandblasting and engraving to achieve the effects that you require and it is also feasible to paint on the embryo to introduce new colours. Many artists use ceramic enamels for this, but they can be difficult to handle as you reheat the bubble when you are finishing the piece. A mixture of powdered coloured glass and gum arabic, blended to a creamy consistency, may be painted on to the surface with little trouble. When the bubble has been decorated to your satisfaction it will need to be reheated and to reheat the embryo a top-loading kiln is almost essential. The embryo is going to be reattached to the blowing iron when it is hot and so it needs to be positioned in the kiln appropriately. We use a number of ceramic rings about 10cm (4in) in diameter. These may be purchased from your kiln supplier, but if they are not available it is probable that some other and equally useful kiln furniture will be purchasable. Place a ring on the floor of the kiln; if you are using a kiln shelf, set it very low down. Place the embryo on the ring so that the hole is pointing vertically upwards. Heat the embryo gradually over 3 to 4hr and then leave the bubble at around 560°C (1,040°F) for about another hour. The embryo then needs to be picked up on a blowing iron. To prepare the iron, gather a small amount of molten glass on to its tip and hold the iron vertically so that the molten glass runs back down it. Thumb a bubble into the iron and, with luck, the glass will burst. If it does not, gently tap the paper-thin bubble downwards on to the floor. Put the iron back to the glory hole and round off the rough edges and then take the iron back to the bench and force a little of the glass that is down the sides of the iron forwards. Form this glass into a doughnut-like pad at the end of the iron. Open up the kiln and stick the doughnut of clear glass that you have just prepared to the rim of the bubble. Wait for a second or two to let the bubble and doughnut pad fuse together, take the embryo out of the kiln with the blowing iron, and, as you shut the kiln lid, turn the iron round so that the embryo is vertically upwards. Get to the glory hole as quickly as you can, stand to one side of it and hold the iron in front of the heat. Do this for a few seconds to get a little heat in to the iron end of the bubble. Remember to keep turning all the

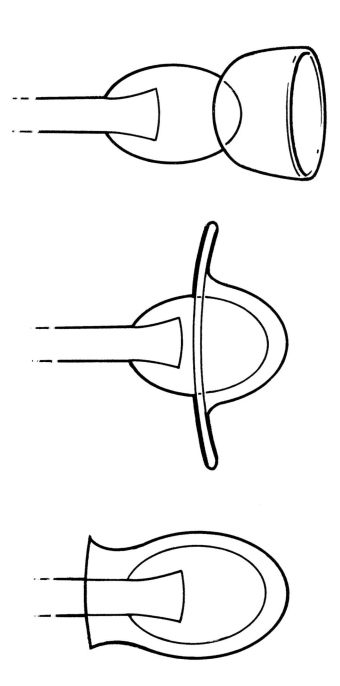

TOP: **The cup is joined to the post.**

MIDDLE: **Opening the cup over the post.**

BOTTOM: **The overlay complete.**

125

time. Carefully move to your regular position at the front of the glory hole and slowly put the embryo into the heat; you will need to work at reheating since it may well take a long time.

The surface of the embryo needs to be completely smooth and round before you can begin to blow the final shape. It may be blown as it is or you can gather more glass on top. In either case you will need to be careful when blowing the object because you have created many thick and thin wall variations during the engraving and sandblasting, as well as almost certainly having some hard and soft colour problems. In general, when you have a piece with many hot spots and weak spots, remember to keep it hot; there is a great temptation to work the glass at a colder than normal temperature but the exact opposite is what is required. Try not to do too much at one time, take short steps as you progress to the finished shape, but do keep it hot at all times.

I use the fluid lines that the graal technique creates to bring life to children's drawings: by using graal in combination with incalmo, layers of blue sky and green land are placed on either side of the characters. In another series of my work, known as 'Only Words', both graal and incalmo techniques were used: a series of coloured rings are sandblasted in the graal technique, with one word repeated several times on each; three or four words are put together to make a phrase, the rings are then warmed up in a top-loading kiln and put together using the incalmo technique – simple, bold messages in bold colours on simple shapes.

Ed Burke: MY FAMILY.

Ed Burke: C'EST LA VIE.

Torching

This is a way of decorating glass while it is still hot. You will need to warm up some rod colour to draw out into colour canes; pick up the preheated colour on a punty iron, with a small amount of hot glass from the furnace. Get the coloured glass hot in the glory hole and then marver it to a finger shape; take the finger of glass back to the glory hole and warm up the tip. Come away from the glory hole and grip as small an amount of the hot finger tip as you can with tweezers. Slowly pull a thread of glass from the colour and place it on the floor; after a few seconds the glass will be cool enough to touch then break it up into useful lengths about 40cm (16in) long.

Now that you have prepared the colour canes you can gather the glass to make the object. Allow it to cool a little and ask your assistant to take it from you. Meanwhile, set up a small, hand-held gas torch, such as you would use for welding or braising. Ask your assistant to cease turning the post. Point the flame of

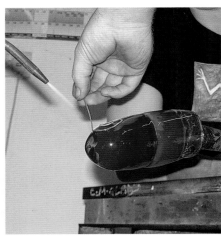

ABOVE: **Drawing intricate designs using the torch.**

LEFT: **Ed Burke:** FLIM FLAM.

the torch on to the tip of one of the colour canes and soften it; you can now draw on to the gather of glass with the molten coloured glass cane by employing a method similar to that used with wood glue when making a sandblasting mask. This is a wonderfully direct way of drawing on glass and well worth the time it takes to learn. The glass can be gathered on or blown to shape from its current size, but be careful and watch out for hot

and cold colour movements. The golden rule when you have hard and soft colours next to each other on the same piece of glass is to make the whole work really hot and to keep it so.

My 'Flim Flam' series involved extensive torched cane work. These pieces also make use of the incalmo technique to put a band of colour around the top of them; in the typical style the pieces have bold contrasting colours on simple shapes.

Mark Locock: VASES.

Optic Mould

Optic moulds come in several shapes and sizes and are put to a number of uses. They are generally made from cast iron, although there are lighter ones made of aluminium. They are cylindrical in shape, with a bullet-shaped hole in the centre. Around the edges of the hole there will be a series of ridges. Sometimes the ridges are quite angular and others are curved. Some moulds have a hole at the bottom and others do not. The number of ridges may vary from as few as six up to many dozens. In its most basic use the mould creates an optical effect of light and dark.

A gather of glass is shaped to approximately the shape and size of the hole down the centre of the mould and then a small air bubble is put into the glass. The gather is reheated slightly and then put into the mould. While the glass is there, the glass-maker blows down the pipe, forcing the glass into the ridges. Because the bubble is round on the inside and ridged on the outside you now have a bubble with bands of thick and thin glass travelling down its length. As the glass is blown to its final shape, this will catch the light creating the illusion of light and shade. This can be further emphasized by using rod colour inside the gather before employing the optic mould.

After the glass has been blown into the mould some interesting effects can be created by twisting up the gather. Warm up the gather in the glory hole and then jack down a small marble at the end. Reheat the glass again and this time grasp the glass at the cut-down point with diamond shears. Roll the iron up the bench while you hold the tip of the glass and the ridges will begin to spiral up. Knock the marble off the end and then heat the glass thoroughly before blowing it up.

Another common use for optic moulds is to pick up coloured canes. Stretch a series of canes as you would for torching and then cut them to the length of the optic mould. Place a cane between each of the ridges and then drop the hot gathered glass into the mould as before. Sometimes the canes will break from the heat of the gather and so, to avoid this, the mould may either be placed inside the top-loading kiln or on to a hot plate to warm up the canes first. Once the canes have been melted on to the sides of the post they can be spiralled up if required. You need not use only one colour of cane, you could use many that repeat themselves round the side, or the colours could be completely randomly used.

A series of spots can be put on to the surface by using the trailing technique in conjunction with the optic mould. Make a ridged post while your assistant prepares a finger of colour. Stick the tip of the finger on to the waste glass at the top of the post. Then, with one long roll down the length of the bench, trail a spiral down the sides of the post. The trail will stick only to the peaks of the ridges. Take the glass to the glory hole and heat it through. As the glass gets hotter the parts of the trail that are not touching the post will melt and snap, leaving small dots of colour on the ridges. You can, of course, spiral this up also. Another possibility is to lay on another trail of a different colour in between the lines of the first one before you melt it in. This will create spots in two colours.

Cane Work

These techniques, known as latticino and reticello, are extremely fine glass blowing styles originating from Venice. Previously made canes are used to create intricate vessels with spiralling or criss-crossing lines, generally in white opal glass on clear. Each of the different names – latticino, filigrana and reticello, refers to a specific pattern. Latticino is an Italian word that translates as 'little milk-white glass strands'. Latticino vessels are generally clear with many thin white spirals over them. Filigrana is a variation on the same theme. Reticello is again similar to latticino but has white spirals overlapping in two different directions. The crossing of the two sets of spirals creates little diamond shapes, often with a small air bubble inside.

Preparing the canes needs to be done with great care and attention, badly prepared ones will show in the final piece. Pick up some white rod glass on a punty iron and warm it through. Shape it to a cylinder and let it cool; gather clear glass over the top of the colour, being careful to not pick up too much. Again shape the glass on the punty to a cylindrical shape, but do it in such a way that there is not too much clear glass at the end. Now get your assistant to make a crown punty to the same width as your cased white glass, dip the tip of your glass into water and then heat it up as much as you can in the glory hole. Ask your assistant to put the back of his iron on to the floor, with the crown punty pointing upwards. Come from the glory hole to your assistant and allow the bottom of your glass to land on to the punty, as if you were bringing a foot bit to be placed on a stem. By using your combined judgement, you and your assistant should move your irons to a horizontal position. Both of you need to turn the irons as you walk backwards away from each other. As the canes reach the required length and thickness, lay the irons on the floor and remove the glass with a wet file at each end.

These white canes are cased in clear glass so that, if you place them side by side, you create a series of alternate clear and white stripes.

The optic mould.

Putting the glass into the optic mould.

Allowing the glass to set.

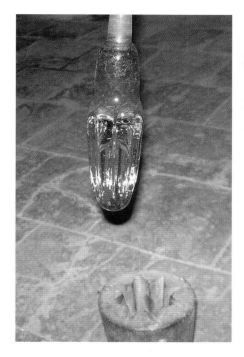

Taking the glass from the optic mould.

Twisting the optic post.

Canes on a cane marver.

glory hole and warm them through; jack the tube down when you are back at the bench to create a bubble and knock the waste piece of glass from the end of the bubble. As you are closing the bubble, you may wish to put a twist on to the canes. This can be done with the jacks, but I recommend that you should use diamond shears, as in the optic mould techniques. Once the spirals have been created from the canes they can either be covered over with a fresh clear gather or blown to the final shape from the canes alone.

Reticello, the fishnet pattern, can be created in a number of ways. Make up a white and clear spiral post as explained above, and ask your assistant to prepare a finger of solid white colour and then to thread it on top of the post so that it spirals in the opposite way. Another method is to blow the first twisted post into a small cup; remove it from the punty and place it into a top-loading kiln, rim-side uppermost. Make another twisted post on another blowing iron with more canes, but this time twist them in the opposite direction from the first post. Warm the second post up at the glory hole and then place it inside the first cup which is in the kiln; take the two to the glory hole to even out the temperatures before you blow the glass to shape.

Canes in an optic mould.

To make a latticino vessel you will need to place a number of cased canes onto a cane marver (this is a metal plate with ridges on it, it looks rather like an optic mould that has been rolled out flat) and then put the marver on to the hot plate. Measure the width of all the canes laid side by side; divide the distance by three and then set a calliper to that distance; a 'pi divider' may be used to work out your dimensions for you. Gather some clear glass on a blowing iron and hold it upwards, so that the glass falls backwards on to the iron sides. Quickly thumb a bubble into the glass and, with luck, the thin film of glass on the end of the iron will burst. If the glass does not burst, tap the bubble on to the floor and burst it that way. Reheat the glass in the glory hole; make the resulting doughnut to the size set on the callipers. Take the gather to the hot plate and roll the glass on to one end of the warmed canes very slowly; take the tube of canes to the

GLOSSARY

Italicized terms have individual entries in the glossary.

Acid etching Process of etching the surface of glass with *hydrofluoric acid*. Acid-etched decoration is produced by covering the glass with an acid-resistant substance, such as wax, through which the design is scratched. A mixture of dilute hydrofluoric acid and potassium fluoride is then applied to etch the exposed areas.

Acid polishing Process of making a glossy, polished surface by dipping the object glass into a mixture of hydrofluoric and sulphuric acid.

Air marver Moving the piece while on the pipe or *punty* to let the molten glass flow without shaping it against a *marver*, paper pad or block.

Air stem, air twist A long, thin bubble, or more usually multiple bubbles, in the stem of a goblet. They may be created separately, stored and applied to a goblet.

Air trap A bubble surrounded by glass; it can be created by pushing a recess into the glass and casing over with more molten glass.

Alkali In glass-making, a soluble salt consisting mainly of potassium carbonate or sodium carbonate; an essential ingredient of glass, generally accounting for about 15 to 20 per cent by weight of the batch.

Annealing Process of slowly cooling a completed object in an auxiliary part of the glass furnace or in a separate furnace. Strained glasses break easily if they are subjected to mechanical or thermal shock.

Applied decoration Heated glass elements (such as *canes*, *murrini*, and *trails*) applied during manufacture to a glass object that is still hot.

Baluster Type of English drinking glass of the late seventeenth and eighteenth centuries, with the stem in the form of a baluster.

Bar Single piece of glass formed by fusing several canes or rods. A bar may be cut into numerous slices, all with the same design, to be used as inlays or appliqués, or in making mosaic glass.

Batch Glass is made from a mixture (batch) of chemicals; common examples are: sand, lime, limestone (calcium carbonate), soda (sodium carbonate), soda ash, lithium carbonate, feldspar, sodium nitrate, zinc oxide, barium carbonate, fluorspar and antimony oxide.

Battledore Glass-worker's tool in the form of a square, wooden paddle with a handle; it is used to smooth the bottom of a vessel or other object.

Beeswax Used to lubricate jacks and other tools.

Blank Any cooled glass object that requires further forming or decoration to be finished.

Blobbing Technique of decorating hot glass by dropping on to its surface blobs of molten glass, usually of a different colour or colours.

Blocks Pieces of fruit wood, most commonly cherry but also pear and apple, carved to a shape useful in forming glass and then soaked until they are waterlogged.

Blowing Technique of forming an object by inflating a gob of molten glass gathered on the end of a *blowpipe*.

Blowpipe An iron or steel tube, usually about 1.5m (5ft) long, for blowing glass.

Brilliant-cut glass Objects with elaborate, deeply cut patterns that usually cover the entire surface and are highly polished.

Bubble A pocket of gas trapped in glass during its manufacture. The term is used for both bubbles introduced intentionally (also known as *air traps* or beads) and those trapped accidentally during the melting process. Very small bubbles are known as *seeds*.

Bull's-eye A glass pane with a *punty* mark surrounded by concentric ridges. This was the central part of a large pane of crown glass.

Button Small blob of glass applied direct to the centre bottom of a piece and flattened there, usually to provide a thicker point for applying the *punty* and for grinding away the punty mark.

Cameo glass Glass of one layer covered, usually by casing, with one or more layers of contrasting colours. The outer layers are acid-etched, carved, cut or engraved to produce a design that stands out from the background.

Cane A thin, coloured rod, or a composite coloured rod consisting of groups of rods of different colours bundled together and fused.

Casing The application of a layer of glass over one of a contrasting colour.

Castable Shorthand name for high-temperature refractory materials that are in powder form, mixed with water and poured into a mould.

Casting Name for a wide variety of techniques used to form glass in a mould.

Ceramic fibre blanket Modern industrial high-temperature insulation to replace the much more dangerous asbestos.

Chair Bench used by the *gaffer* while forming a glass object; can also refer to the team of workers who assist the gaffer.

Clamp Tool sometimes used instead of a *punty* to hold the closed end of a partly formed glass vessel while the open end is being shaped. Sometimes called the *gadget*.

Copper-wheel engraving Technique of decorating the surface of an object. Copper disks of various sizes and rim profiles are rotated on a spindle; an abrasive, such as carborundum mixed with oil, is applied to the edge of the wheel.

Cold working General name for sandblasting, grinding and polishing glass.

Core The form to which molten glass is applied in order to make a core-formed vessel. In pre-Roman times the core is thought to have been made of animal dung mixed with clay.

Core forming Technique of forming a vessel by trailing or gathering molten glass around a core supported by a rod. After forming, the object is removed from the rod and annealed, after which the core is removed by scraping.

Cracking off Process of detaching a glass object from a *blowpipe* or *punty*.

Crystal Glass with approximately 20–35 per cent lead oxide added.

Cullet Pieces of broken glass.

Cups Blown cup shape used for putting colour on to the outside of an object.

Cutting Removing glass from the surface of an object by grinding it with a rotating wheel made of stone, wood or metal and an abrasive suspended in liquid.

Cylinder glass Window glass made by blowing a cylinder. The cylinder is then detached from the *blowpipe* and both ends are removed; the cylinder is then cut lengthways, reheated and either tooled or allowed to slump until it assumes the form of a flat sheet.

Devitrification When glass is heated, but is still not liquid, and is held at that temperature for too long, white crystals may form on its surface. Once formed, they are impossible to remove.

Diamond-point engraving Technique of decorating glass by scratching the surface with a diamond, introduced by the Venetians in the sixteenth century and carried to some of its greatest artistic heights in the Netherlands during the seventeenth.

Dip mould Cylindrical, one-piece mould open at the top so that the *gather* can be dipped into it and then inflated.

Domed foot Foot in the shape of a hollow hemisphere, usually made separately, like a bowl, and attached to the piece.

Engraving Process of cutting into the surface of an annealed glass object either by holding it against a rotating copper wheel fed with an abrasive, or by scratching it, usually with a diamond. See also *cutting* and *stippling*.

Finishing Process of making an object into its final shape while it is still hot.

Fire polishing The reintroduction of a vessel into the *glory hole* to melt its surface.

Firebrick Brick made to withstand high temperatures.

Flame working Technique of forming objects from rods and tubes of glass which, when heated in a flame, become soft and may be manipulated into the desired shape.

Flashing Application of a very thin layer of glass of one colour over a layer of a contrasting colour; sometimes used as a synonym for *casing*. Flashing is also the term used for a short reheat of glass in the *glory hole*.

Folded foot A thin rim is folded over or under to provide more strength at the rim.

Folded rim A flared rim is folded in or out to make a doubled thickness, thus giving more strength.

Foot Added to the bottom of an object to provide a flat area of support; usually shaped so that only the rim rests on the flat.

Founding Initial phase of melting batch.

Frit Pieces of broken glass bigger than powder but smaller than *cullet*.

Furnace Enclosed structure for the production and application of heat.

Fusing Process of heating pieces of glass in a kiln or *furnace* until they bond.

Julia Linstead: GLASS ENGRAVING.
PHOTO: JOHN DONOGHUE

Julia Linstead: ONE-OFF.
PHOTO: JOHN DONOGHUE

Gadget A metal rod with a spring clip that grips the foot of a vessel and so avoids the use of a *punty*.

Gaffer Colloquial variant of godfather; the master craftsman in charge of a chair, or team, of hot-glass workers.

Gather A mass of molten glass (sometimes called a gob) collected on the end of a *blowpipe, punty* or gathering iron.

Glory hole A hot chamber used to reheat glass during the making process.

Goblet A drinking vessel with a bowl that rests on a stemmed foot.

Graal A technique used in Swedish glass where a flashed or cased cup is annealed and designs are cut into the colour. The cup is then repeated and cased or gathered over.

Hot shop Although sometimes used as a slang term for studio, it most commonly refers to the physical area within a studio or glass factory where the melting and working of furnace glass occurs.

Hydrofluoric acid A highly corrosive acid capable of attacking silicates such as glass; the pure acid dissolves glass, leaving a brilliant, acid-polished surface.

Incalmo Two distinct sections of colour created by opening out two blown pieces then heating and bringing the edges together; the joined piece is then blown to shape.

Iridized glass Prepared by spraying or blowing metallic compounds on to the glass near the end of the blowing process.

Jacks Also known as *pucellas*, the main tools for glass making. These tong-like tools are comprised of two metal blades joined together with a metal bow.

Latticino Spiral lines, usually of white glass, used in stems and on the body of Venetian-style glass, made as cane which is imbedded in the glass while working.

Lead oxide Gives weight to glass and a brilliant reflection when it is cut, it also extends the working range of glass.

Lehr The oven used for annealing glassware.

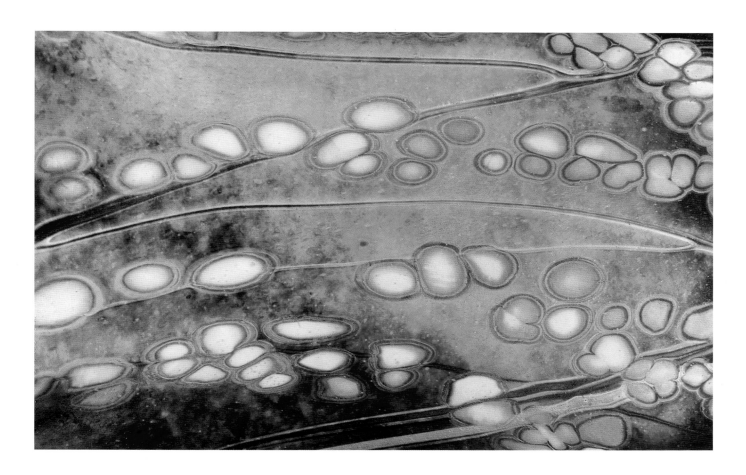

Siddy Langley: CLOSE UP OF IRIDIZED GLASS.

Lime Calcined limestone, which, added to the glass batch in small quantities, gives stability.

Lip wrap A contrasting line of glass added around the lip of a piece just before finishing, often of a contrasting colour.

Looping and dragging The piece is threaded usually with coloured glass. The surface of the glass is dragged with a hooked tool causing the threads to loop.

Marver French *marbre* (marble); a smooth, flat surface which glass is rolled on when it is attached to the *blowpipe* in order to smooth it.

Melt The fluid glass produced by melting a batch of raw materials.

Merese Small disk of glass separating a bowl from a stem, often an ornamental detail on glasses.

Millefiori 'Thousand flowers'; small designs created in *cane* by arranging rods of colour; the rods are then heated and pulled to stretch and reduce the design.

Moile The name for the blob of glass at the end of the pipe before the making of an object is begun.

Mould A form, normally made of wood or metal, used for shaping and/or decorating molten glass.

Murrini Similar to *millefiori* but when the *canes* are cut the cross section will show a picture or a letter.

Newspaper Used, when formed, wetted and held in the hand, for shaping glass, to replace a mould or block.

Optic mould An open mould with a patterned interior.

Parchoffi Similar to *jacks* or *pucellas* but with wooden blades instead of metal.

Parison French *paraison*; a *gather*, on the end of a *blowpipe*, which is already partly inflated.

Polishing Smoothing the surface of an object when it is cold by holding it against a rotating wheel fed with a fine abrasive; glass may also be polished with handheld tools.

Pot A fireclay container placed in the furnace in which the batch of glass ingredients is fused and kept molten.

Potash Potassium carbonate; an alternative to soda as a source of alkali in the manufacture of glass.

Powder Concentrated glass colour in powder form. The powder can be placed on the *marver* so that the hot glass may be rolled in it; the powder melts into the glass, forming a thin layer on the surface.

Pressed glass Results when a hot gather of glass is placed in a mould and a matching metal shape is forced down inside.

Prunt A blob of glass applied to a glass object as decoration.

Pucellas Also known as *jacks*.

Punty or pontil A solid metal rod applied to the base of a vessel to hold it during manufacture.

Reduction The balance of the gas and air mixture in the *glory hole* is critical. If there is more gas in the mixture than normal it is said to be a 'reducing' flame. Reduction is useful in glass-working because it changes some metal oxides to fine particles of metal.

Reflection The property of returning light back toward its source.

Refraction The 'bending' of light when it passes from one medium into another.

Refractory Any material that withstands the high heat needed for melting glass.

Ribs Vertical lines forming waves of glass around a piece.

Sand The most common form of silica used in making glass; it is collected from the seashore or, preferably, from deposits with fewer impurities.

Seeds Minute bubbles of gas, usually occurring in groups.

Shards Very thin glass, usually made by blowing out a bubble and shattering it. It is used to produce thin areas of uniform colour, being picked up like *frit* or *powder*.

Silica Silicon dioxide, the main ingredient of glass; the most common form used in glass making has always been sand.

Slumping The heating of unsupported glass, allowing it to bend freely.

Soda Sodium carbonate (soda) is commonly used as the *alkali* ingredient of glass. It serves as a flux to reduce the fusion point of the batch.

Sodium nitrate An ingredient in glass-making when mixing *batch*.

Stones Small objects in the molten glass.

Striking colour Some colours of glass and other substances will change colour under special conditions.

Tank A large receptacle constructed in a furnace for melting the *batch*.

Threading A thin line of glass wound around the body of the glass.

Trail A thin line of glass across the body, not around it, like threading.

Twist A type of decoration in the stems of eighteenth-century and later drinking glasses, made by twisting a glass rod embedded with threads of white or coloured glass, columns of air or a combination of all three.

Wheel engraving A process of decorating the surface of glass by the grinding action of a wheel, using disks of various size and material.

Zinc oxide An ingredient in glass-making when mixing *batch*.

Paul Barcroft: JALAPENO VASES.

INDEX